WHISKY WALKS
SCOTLAND

THE MOST SATISFYING WAY TO DISCOVER SCOTLAND

TABLE OF CONTENT

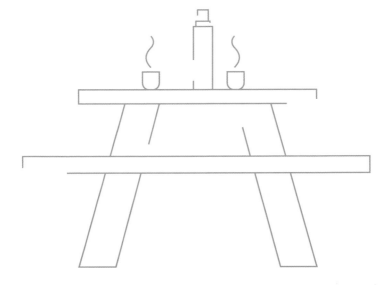

1

INTRODUCTION

ABOUT THE AUTHOR

You know those people who are most comfortable at home in a comfy chair with their eyes glued to a book? And if they move away from the book it is only to walk through a tranquil forest enjoying the solitude and the surrounding nature? That's me!

Unless I get one of my adventurous fits. When I get one of those I am off as soon as I can, and then my introvert nature takes the back seat for a while, because exploring is one of my great passions. I love experiencing foreign cultures, fascinating nature, and delicious food, and this you can only do when embracing the whole experience, introvertedness be damned.

I am the daughter of anthropologists and spent part of my childhood in what I remember as a life resembling the *Indiana Jones* movies: attending strange exorcisms by night, dodging venomous scorpions and snakes, crossing cliffs on weathered ropes, and eating exotic spiced food. Like all kids I blame my parents for everything, and that includes my need for adventure.

When I'm not travelling, I'm hiding at home in Denmark, exploring the forests, writing stories that might or might not be published some day, who knows. Married and with three kids, I find it best to face life with a bit of humour, as you will probably find out when you read this book.

ABOUT THE BOOK

What can be more satisfying than enjoying a dram of whisky after a long day of walking? That feeling of coming inside after experiencing the rough cold wind, feeling the liquid warming your entire body as you swallow the first sip and it runs down your throat – it is simply glorious, and it is the reason behind this book.

Making Scotland the destination was for me an obvious choice. Temperamental weather, majestic mountains, glorious nature, and *Uisge Beatha* (water of life), as whisky is called in Gaelic.

This book is meant to be an adventure, not a lecture about whisky or how it is made. There will be no fancy whisky slang and there will be no snobbishness in regards to brand, age, and geographic position of the distilleries. What there will be is plenty of mouth-watering whiskies or, if the distillery hasn't yet cracked open the cask, then gin, spirits, or aqua vitae. Most of the whiskies in the book are single malt, but sometimes you come across something else that is just as brilliant.

I have chosen the distilleries I describe because they are independent and/or small and locally run. But although I endeavoured to stay clear of all the 'big boys', there are plenty of them along the way if you should feel like visiting them. It can be enlightening to get the perspective of both worlds. When first you look at all the distilleries there are in Scotland it seems like there are too many to count, but if you take away all the big distilleries there aren't that many left. This is why I have chosen to add whisky bars and whisky experiences to the book as well; that way there will be more options to choose from when you go on your adventure.

You know how people say that the Scottish are stingy? This is of course not true. However, they like to make sure nothing goes to waste. When it comes to whisky, they are no different. All of the distilleries in the book try to minimise their waste and to benefit the community as best they can. An example of this is the leftover draff. The barley, after being used, is given to local farmers to feed their cattle. The draff has many vital vitamins in it that are beneficial for cattle. Also, many distilleries use water streams to produce electricity in order to become more and more self-sufficient and ecologically conscious. New distilleries are being built around Scotland, creating new jobs and creating new life in small towns and in remote locations. It has been a joy to see the locals' support and enthusiasm for these endeavours.

2

BEFORE SETTING OFF

CHOOSE A WALK OR A WHISKY

HIKE LOCATION ————————→

NAME OF THE WHISKY ————→

INFORMATION
ABOUT THE WHISKY ←————

INFORMATION
ABOUT THE HIKE ←————

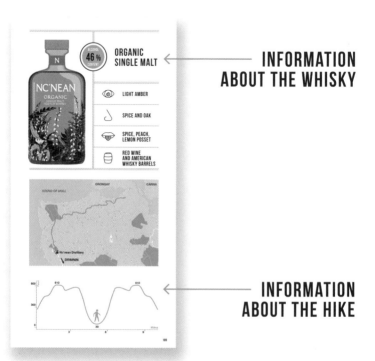

WHISKY RATING

I am of the belief that there is a whisky out there for everyone (and for every occasion). But please keep in mind that taste differs from person to person. In this book I will be sharing my opinion about the different whiskies, but they might not be to your taste. Do not despair, there is sure to be a whisky you like somewhere in Scotland. That is the beauty of a whisky trip: You get to explore all the different kinds of whisky and find that very special one that you enjoy. If you don't like whisky at all but are travelling with someone who does, rest at ease, there are plenty of other drinks you can enjoy in Scotland.

TRAIL DIFFICULTY RATING

There should be a walk for everyone in this book. The challenge has been to find great walks that end up at a distillery or at the perfect whisky bar. There are obviously not that many distilleries and bars on the top of a mountain. But what you can be sure of is that they are always close to a stream or a river, as water is one of the main ingredients in whisky. And who doesn't like a lovely walk along a riverside?

So, whether you are young or old, in good or bad shape, there is a walk for you. There are exceptionally long walks for those who like a whole day in the wilderness, and there are short walks for those of you who like to do a bit of sightseeing while having a light stroll.

The walks are divided into three categories:

WALKING

easy to moderate

HIKING

moderate to difficult

MOUNTAIN HIKING

difficult; difficult sometimes depending on the weather

PREPARING FOR YOUR HIKES

ALWAYS BRING TOILET PAPER

Experienced travellers might already know that panicky feeling you get when you are stuck in the middle of nowhere and you just have to go to the toilet. If you are lucky you only need to pee; if you are not so lucky foreign food might have turned your stomach upside down and you are dealing with what we call a 'Delhi Belly'. I sincerely hope you will not experience the latter, and if you do there is no advice other than 'just stay strong'. Regardless, you will at some point need to pee and there will not be a toilet anywhere in sight. Now my advice is always, and I mean always, bring toilet paper with you. You never know when it might come in handy. Also make sure you bring a waste bag for the used toilet paper.

FOOD AND WATER

Even if you are only going on a small walk, it is always a good idea to bring a snack, something that will give you the energy you need. And it goes without saying that you should bring water. I cannot count the times when I have left without bringing water with me and regretted it. I suggest you always pack food for a whole day. If you are doing a trip that will take the whole day, pack as if you will be gone for two. Always be on the safe side, that way you won't go hungry or thirsty.

For every walk, I will let you know if you should bring lunch or if there is a café or restaurant along the way. Please mind that the restaurants are not always open even if it says so on the door or on their website. Therefore, it is always a good idea to bring something to eat with you.

WASTE BAG

Scotland has absolutely stunning nature, and it is important that we take care of it, so remember not to drop any waste on your walks. Bring a waste bag with you.

CLOTHES

Whatever you think the weather might be like before you head out, think again. In an instant the weather can change, so pack extra clothes for when you get cold or soaked, and wear layers. Especially in spring, summer, and autumn the weather can take you by surprise, going from warm, to wet, to cold.

It is always a good idea to make sure your gear is waterproof, but I have experienced even the most waterproofed equipment succumb to the Scottish weather. Make sure to have extra shoes and clothes with you and try to keep the water out of your backpack.

During the summer the sun can be fierce, so it is a good idea to bring a hat with you. Sunstroke is the last thing you want to experience on a walk. You should also bring some sort of midge protection such as insect repellent, or a net to put over your hat.

FIRST AID KIT AND TOOLS

None of the walks in this book should get you lost, and the likelihood of you being isolated and with no other people near to hear you call out is slim – but you never know. I suggest you bring a multitool, just in case, a first aid kit, matches, a compass, a small torch, and a whistle. Make sure you pack so you don't find yourself in a situation where you regret not bringing it. And make sure to put the most important things in a waterproof bag or container.

PROTECTION AGAINST MIDGES

Nobody said it would be a breeze to travel in Scotland. The weather can be harsh and ever changing, and one would think that travelling during high summer would be best because then there would be less rain. You do get really amazing, sunny summers in Scotland. On the days when the heat is too much you can just go for a walk in the forest. The trees will give you the needed shade. But this is also where the midges will attack you. The bites are of course itchy, but it is the constant buzz around your face, the midges flying into your eyes, ears, and nose that makes one go crazy. The most sensible thing would be to just not be out and about when the midges are at their worst, but then we would stay locked up all summer, and where is the fun in that? If you are going for a walk during summer in the forest or by a lake, make sure to wear clothes that can cover you completely and a hat with net on it, and that you have some repellent (bought or home-made with lavender or citrus) on you. Good luck!

HEALTH AND SAFETY

You are almost ready for your great adventure now. But as the finishing touches are made to this book, the coronavirus has completely changed the world in comparison to when I started writing it. Please remember to check if the distilleries and hotels are open before you visit. Some might have special restrictions. It is important to prioritise your and other people's health when heading off on your whisky adventure. Check the info regarding travelling restrictions that your local government provides.

Safe travels!

MAP AND WALKS

In your preparation for departure you will most likely make the choice to take some form of map with you. Perhaps you like the old-school maps, the sound of thick paper crackling each time you unfold it to find your way on your adventure. In this modern age you can forego the old paper maps and feel the freedom of being guided by an app, perhaps attached to your wrist in the shape of a watch, or maybe you prefer your mobile phone to guide you. Or, perhaps you are like me, totally lost despite countless gadgets and paper maps, and you will need to bring a "master of navigation" (in my case, my husband). The choice is all yours.

When you buy this book you can also get the GPX files of all the walks. The files can be opened and used by many different apps; I used Suunto but there are many different navigation devices out there. If you want to go old school, there is a wide range of maps of Scotland that can easily be bought online or in stores where you would normally buy your maps. The Ordnance Survey is the national mapping agency for Great Britain; they have maps that cover all of Scotland and you can buy them online. If you prefer to go both ways and look at old-fashioned maps, but on a gadget or app, you can also subscribe to the OS maps and access all their maps of Great Britain any time you want.

3

THE WHISKY WALKS

COASTAL CAVE

BRACE YOURSELF FOR A STUNNING COASTAL VIEW, FIERCE WIND, AND A HISTORIC CAVE.

▷ STARTING POINT

KINGSBARNS DISTILLERY

✕ DESTINATION

KINGSBARNS DISTILLERY

🏷 WHISKY

DREAM TO DRAM

卍 DIFFICULTY

HIKING

☆ HIGHLIGHTS

FIFE NESS LIGHTHOUSE, CONSTANTINE'S CAVE, MARKINGS OF THE CRANE BASE BY THE COAST, REMNANTS OF THE OLD HARBOUR AT FIFE NESS

⊘ DURATION OF THE HIKE

3.5 HOURS
7.6 MILES (12.2KM)

△ ELEVATION GAIN

545 FEET
(166M)

ALCOHOL
46 %
CONTENT

SINGLE MALT

GOLDEN

MALT CITRUS
NOTES

CARAMEL CITRUS

BOURBON
AND WINE

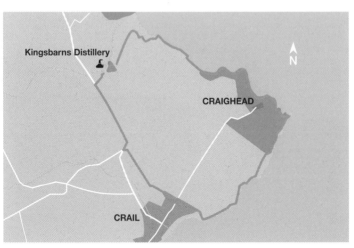

Kingsbarns Distillery

CRAIGHEAD

CRAIL

N

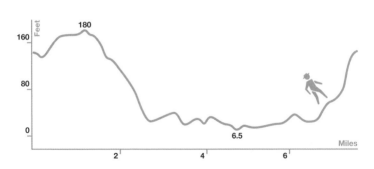

DESCRIPTION OF THE WALK

This hike is set in the picturesque landscape of Fife. It's what I like to call a 'flat walk', one with hardly any slopes; but do not be fooled, there are plenty of challenges on this trip. This very diverse walk takes you through narrow paths in lush fields, up and down bumpy footpaths, onto a rocky beach, past determined golfers, and into a dark cave filled to the brim with bloody history. But the most important thing is that (once you have completed this walk, and your hair resembles a wild bird's nest from the strong wind, and you've endured the incredulous stares of the golfers, as well as having dodged the odd golf ball flying just above your head) you end up at an amazing distillery, where there is warmth, food (if you haven't already eaten), and above all great whisky to make you feel completely warm again.

It is said that Constantine's Cave is the place where Constantine II of Scotland (reigned 900–943) died. According to legend he was killed by Vikings. (Danes, or so they say. Really could just as well have been the Norwegians, they are just as naughty, honestly.) Inside the cave there are Celtic-style drawings of animals on the walls, and outside there is a sign with the history of the cave.

Once you reach the golfing area, please be mindful of golf balls coming your way. Depending on the wind (and the talent of the golfer) you might experience the odd ball or two flying your way. Just stay on the outside of the red poles that are lined up along the golf courses and you should be fine. Make sure you have enough clothes with you, even if you do this walk in summer, because the Scottish weather can be somewhat unpredictable even this far south. Although there is a hotel en route that boasts about serving food from 12pm, I recommend bringing your own picnic (or eating at the distillery café), as the opening hours of pubs and hotels in remote areas can be just as unpredictable as the weather. This walk is good for all kinds of weather but please be aware of tide times before you start off.

Set off from the distillery parking lot. It's a free parking lot, but if you like, you can just pop into the distillery reception and let them know that you will be going on a walk before, or after, visiting the distillery.

You set off down the same road you came from by car, but take a left up a path towards the main road. This main road has a lot of traffic, so please be careful. Before you know it, you are walking along beautiful fields and then you reach the sea. If you don't like walking through the caravan area you can try walking down by the beach if the water level permits it. From here on you keep on following the coastline until you close in on the distillery. Make sure you take that left turn up and away from the golf course at the end, and before you know it, it is whisky time!

TIP

You will probably stumble upon more golfers than Vikings on this walk. If you meet any golfers and they give you an odd look, just smile and wave. They do not always understand why people are walking and not playing golf.

TURN BY TURN DIRECTIONS

Start from the distillery parking lot.

1. Walk back up the road where you came from. Take a left and walk for 0.19 miles along the road.
2. At 0.33 miles you reach the main road. Cross it and take a left and walk on.
3. At 1.21 miles cross the road to the left and follow the narrow path along the field.
4. At 1.97 miles you will reach a small town by the sea.
5. At 2.16 miles, by the hotel, take a left and then a right at 2.22 miles down a gravel road towards the beach.
6. At 2.62 miles you reach a green area overlooking the ocean. This is a good spot for lunch.
7. Go left into the caravan park area. Walk through this area.
8. At 3.32 miles you exit the caravan area. The road turns into a path; follow it through all its bumps, twists, and crannies until you reach Fife Ness lighthouse at 4.39 miles. Climb around it and continue along the coastal line.
9. At 4.91 miles you reach Constantine's Cave.
10. Continue a few steps further till you reach the borders of the golf lodge and walk right following the narrow path along the coast. It is important that you stay on the designated path and do not walk on the golf course or beach.
11. At 6.65 miles head left and up over the fence via the wooden steps and then turn left and walk along the path. The path changes from path to a cemented path.
12. At 6.84 miles take the left path and continue.
13. At 7.04 miles turn left.
14. At 7.09 miles turn left and walk through the gate. Take a left again and walk towards the path straight ahead.
15. Follow that path and then at 7.59 miles you arrive at the distillery once more.

KINGSBARNS DISTILLERY

Kingsbarns Distillery is a family dream come true for brother and sister William and Isabella Wemyss. They are pursuing their dream of distilling single malt whisky in the beautiful Fife area. The distillery is among the newest in Scotland and is nestled in between lush fields and delightful golf courses. It is open 7 days a week and if you want to make sure your trip is not in vain, call and book your visit in advance or book online. They offer several different tours and if you don't have time for a grand tour around the premises, they also offer a flight of whiskies in the café.

The whisky tastes light, fruity, and floral, just as a lowland malt should be. Their new whisky Dream to Dram is the quintessential Kingsbarns spirit embodied both in the flavour and smell. The packaging shows that spirit as well, with a unique pigeon motif that represents the dovecot which is placed in the heart of the distillery. It is clear that a lot of thought and effort has been put into this new whisky.

The Kingsbarns Distillery has a shop that sells both gin and whisky, and a café with tasty sandwiches and delicious cakes, so if you haven't packed lunch, fear not, you will not leave hungry.

DRIVING DIRECTIONS

Off the A917 from St. Andrews drive through the village of Kingsbarns and then down Station Road and you find the distillery.

PRACTICAL INFORMATION

DISTILLERY / WHISKY BAR
KINGSBARNS DISTILLERY & VISITOR CENTRE
East Newhall Farm,
Kingsbarns
Fife, KY16 8QE
+44 (0) 1333 451300
info@kingsbarnsdistillery.com
www.kingsbarnsdistillery.com

RESTAURANT / CAFÉ
KINGSBARNS DISTILLERY
(see information above)

MORE INFORMATION ABOUT THE AREA
KINGDOM HOUSE
Kingdom Avenue,
Glenrothes
Fife, KY7 5LT
+44 (0) 3451 555555
promoting.fife@fife.gov.uk
www.welcometofife.com

ACCOMMODATION OPTION
SYKES COTTAGES LTD
Head office: One City Place
Chester
Cheshire, CH1 3BQ
+44 (0) 1244 356666
www.sykescottages.co.uk
info@sykescottages.co.uk

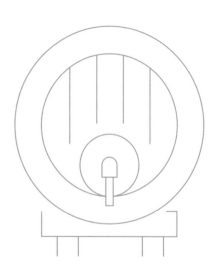

WOODLAND CEMETERY

WHAT COULD BE BETTER THAN A BRISK WINDY WALK
FOLLOWED BY A WHISKY TASTING PAIRED WITH CHOCOLATE?

▷ STARTING POINT

TULLIBARDINE DISTILLERY

✕ DESTINATION

TULLIBARDINE DISTILLERY

🏷 WHISKY

TULLIBARDINE
20 YO

🔲 DIFFICULTY

WALKING

☆ HIGHLIGHTS

BLACKFORD TOWN,
THE OLD CEMETERY,
VIEWPOINT WITH
THE BENCH,
THE NEW RAILROAD BRIDGE

🕑 DURATION OF THE HIKE

1 HOUR
2.5 MILES (4.1KM)

⌒ ELEVATION GAIN

187 FEET
(57M)

ALCOHOL
43 %
CONTENT

SINGLE MALT

Tullibardine
HIGHLAND SINGLE MALT
SCOTCH WHISKY
aged **20** years
DISTILLED AND BOTTLED IN SCOTLAND

'A drop of pure Highland Gold'

PRODUCT OF SCOTLAND

👁	**DARK GOLD**
👃	**VANILLA BUTTERSCOTCH ALLSPICE**
👄	**CHOCOLATE, APPLES, ALLSPICE, HONEY**
🛢	**BOURBON**

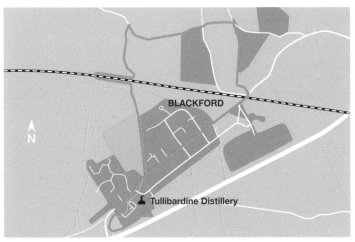

BLACKFORD

⛺ Tullibardine Distillery

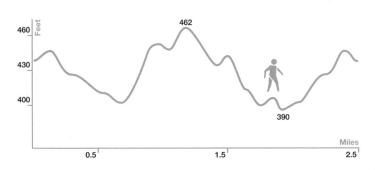

DESCRIPTION OF THE WALK

This is a gorgeous little walk. You get to see the small town of Blackford, woodland, an old cemetery, and the best view of the area when you reach the viewpoint. I recommend bringing your own lunch on this trip, as the distillery does not have a café. Although the town does have pubs and a hotel, none of them were open when I was last there. But the viewpoint of the walk is the perfect place for a picnic. This walk can be done in all sorts of weather.

Situated right next to the A9 and nestled in between mountains and fields, in the south-east of Perthshire, this area is the perfect place for a distillery. Although the mountains look amazing and seem close by, they are in fact quite a way away from the distillery and so I chose the walk that can be done from the distillery. Fortunately, this walk also provides you with stunning views of both mountains and fields, so it's a win-win. Let the distillery know that you have parked on their parking lot and when you expect to be back for your whisky tour.

The route I chose requires you to walk past the old cemetery, but for those who like looking at old graves, I would recommend taking a look at the cemetery. There are graves there that date back to the 17th century and the old church ruins look picturesque on the hillside.

When you continue your walk away from the church and up the pavement road there will be a great photo opportunity of the old church ruin and the mountains on the other side of the distillery.
At this point you can also cut the walk short should you need to. Simply take a left and walk towards the church (having the church on your left and the woods on the right side) and this road will lead you back to the railway crossing and Blackford. As the weather can be unpredictable in Scotland sometimes, a backup plan like that might be smart.

However, if you are up for it, continue onwards and take advantage of all the great viewpoints on the way, especially on the top of the small hill with the bench. This is a great place for a picnic. The rest of the walk is easy, going over the new railway bridge and back into town, where a great whisky experience awaits you.

TIP

If you can, try the Murray Marsala cask finish. With its spicy aroma, plump fruits, and smooth orange finish, it makes for a delicious treat.

TURN BY TURN DIRECTIONS

Start from the parking lot at the distillery.

1. Walk back up the road where you came from. Take a right and walk through the small town.
2. At 0.76 miles you will reach the railway crossing; after this, walk left up the path towards Gleneagle Road.
3. At 0.83 miles you reach the old churchyard. Go right towards the woods.
4. At 0.87 miles follow the path or road with the woods on your right side and cemetery and field on your left side.
5. At 1.04 miles walk left up the road. Please mind the cars.
6. At 1.43 miles go left through the wooden gate and uphill. On the top there is a viewpoint and a bench. This is a perfect place for lunch break.
7. Follow the path and walk through another wooden gate.
8. Follow the path downhill and take a right towards the railroad bridge.
9. At 1.76 miles head up the stairs of the bridge and down on the other side. Take a left and walk with the railway on your left and the river on your right.
10. At 1.90 miles take a right towards the little bridge and cross the river. Follow the path up to town.
11. At 2.21 miles you reach the end of the road; take a right and follow the road until you reach the distillery.
12. At 2.49 miles you are back at the distillery.

TULLIBARDINE DISTILLERY

Tullibardine Distillery's history goes back a long way, as far as the 15th century when King James IV graced the premises with a visit. The king loved beer so much that he stopped here before his coronation to buy some. Back then the location was used for brewing beer from the same source of water that they distil whisky from today.

Today the distillery is distilling whisky the old-fashioned way. The staff matures and bottles all whisky on the premises. Tours are available 7 days a week from 10am to 5pm, and although you might get lucky, it is advisable to book in advance.

One of the great things about Tullibardine Distillery is that they do a chocolate tour. It's a 90-minute tour that cost £25 when I visited, and it is absolutely worth it. The setting where you have the tasting is very classy and the whisky and chocolate samples are simply divine. They also offer a classic tour, a bonded tour, and a connoisseur tour.

If you prefer visiting while there isn't a busload of tourists, just give the distillery a call and ask when the best time for a visit will be. Normally it's very early or very late but it differs. They are always happy to answer any questions you may have.

DRIVING DIRECTIONS

Head off the A9, go on the B8081 and down Moray Street and then Stirling Street where you will find the distillery.

PRACTICAL INFORMATION

DISTILLERY / WHISKY BAR
TULLIBARDINE LTD
Blackford
Perth and Kinross, PH4 1QG
+44 (0) 1764 661809
shop.admin@tullibardine.com
www.tullibardine.com

RESTAURANT / CAFÉ
Bring a picnic.

MORE INFORMATION ABOUT THE AREA
PERTH & KINROSS COUNCIL
Pullar House
35 Kinnoull Street,
Perth
Perth and Kinross, PH1 5GD
+44 (0) 1738 475000
enquiries@pkc.gov.uk
www.pkc.gov.uk

ACCOMMODATION OPTION
SYKES COTTAGES LTD
Head office: One City Place
Cheshire, CH1 3BQ
+44 (0) 1244 356666
info@sykescottages.co.uk
www.sykescottages.co.uk

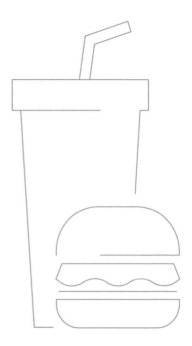

LINDORES ABBEY

'TRANQUILLITY' IS THE KEYWORD FOR THIS WALK.

▷ START AND END POINT

LINDORES ABBEY PARKING LOT

✕ DESTINATION

LINDORES ABBEY DISTILLERY

◈ WHISKY

AQUA VITAE

卍 DIFFICULTY

WALKING

☆ HIGHLIGHTS

THE BEAR MARKED INTO THE FIELD

◷ DURATION OF THE HIKE

2 HOURS
3.8 MILES (6.1KM)

△ ELEVATION GAIN

515 FEET
(157M)

BOTANICAL SPIRIT

ALCOHOL **40 %** CONTENT

👁 CLEAR

👃 HERBAL SWEET

👅 PEAR, CINNAMON, CLOVE, PEACH

🛢 NO CASK

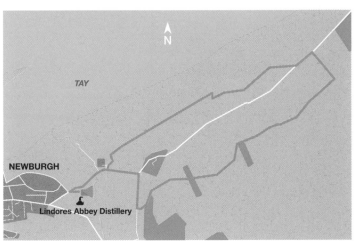

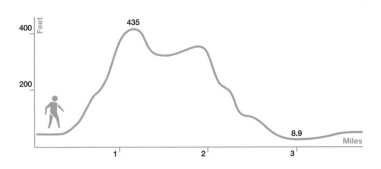

DESCRIPTION OF THE WALK

Depending on where you are from and what the rules of access rights are in your part of the world, this can be a boundary-challenging adventure – but a gorgeous one! You get an amazing view of the coast and the town below, and you get to meet animals along the way.

You can bring your own lunch if you prefer, as there are lots of nice spots to rest, but in town there is a brilliant little coffee shop called East Port Garage and Coffee Shop (do not be discouraged by the name, they will make sure you don't go hungry).

Make sure to let the distillery know that you are parking before or after visiting them, and then head to the right, out of the small town.

The first farm you pass on your left is a farm you will be passing through on your way back, so make a mental note of that. It is the farm further up and to the right that you are heading towards now, and you are entering one of their fenced pastures where there might be horses grazing. With Scotland's nature and walking laws, you are entitled to enter this pasture because it is a path to the forest and the hills. Needless to say, it is always important to behave well when entering other people's properties and to make sure not to disturb or stress the animals.

Follow the turn-by-turn directions and along the way make sure to look to your right to see the big bear that is marked into the field on the hill and famous in this area. You can make a detour and take a closer look at it, or continue to follow the turn-by-turn directions and head further away from the town to enjoy the spectacular views.

You have to go through a lot of gates, but just follow the directions and you are sure to go the right way. When you reach the farm at the end, you are on the right path and it is okay to proceed. Just follow the path and head to the main road and back to the distillery where the peaceful surroundings of the Lindores Abbey await you.

=========================== DID YOU KNOW? ===========================

During the whisky's maturation in the cask at the warehouse, about 0.5 - 2 % of the whisky evaporates per year. This is called the "Angels' Share". Lucky angels they have in Scotland!

TURN BY TURN DIRECTIONS

Start from the parking lot at the distillery.

1. Walk to the right when you exit the parking lot and walk out of town.
2. At 0.40 miles take a right up a gravel road towards the farm.
3. At 0.59 miles after you passed the farm, walk through the gate into a pasture on the left side and head up towards the woods.
4. At the end of the pasture, walk through the gate towards the forest and take a left.
5. At 0.75 miles, when the road forks out into two paths, take the right path upwards.
6. Walk through forest and at 1.12 miles walk downhill to the lower path.
7. At 1.29 miles walk through the gate.
8. At 1.62 miles go through the steel gate and then go left.
9. Walk along the tree line and at 1.92 miles go through the steel gate and then through the red gate to your left.
10. Walk down towards the road and go through the gate.
11. Cross the road and walk left and at 2.14 miles walk through the gate and into the pasture.
12. At 2.21 miles walk through the gate into the next field and walk across and downward and through the gate.
13. Follow the perimeter of the field towards the farm.
14. At 2.77 miles walk slightly right and then left and follow the gravel path.
15. At 3.36 miles you reach the farm. Walk through the gate and head to the main road.
16. At 3.45 miles you are at the main road again. Go right and walk back to the parking lot.
17. At 3.79 miles you reach the distillery.

LINDORES ABBEY DISTILLERY

Prepare to be amazed by the tranquillity that you experience when you enter the front door to Lindores Abbey Distillery. It is amazing. As soon as you step inside you are greeted with tranquil monastic music that resonates with the history and the foundation of the distillery. The distillery was built on the old abbey farm across from the abbey ruins, using as many local materials as possible. Inside, the cloister link leads from the elegant visitor centre through to the stillroom and tells the fascinating story of the abbey. It is probably the most elegant and peaceful distillery visitor centre in Scotland, so make sure you have enough time to enjoy it.

They are open 7 days a week and offer a tour which includes tasting the Aqua Vitae, as well as two other drams. Their own whisky was not ready yet when I visited, but it was maturing peacefully in casks until, hopefully very soon, it is ready to be bottled and sold. Do not let that stop you from visiting the distillery straight away though, as the Aqua Vitae is so delicious that you will want to take a bottle home with you.

DRIVING DIRECTIONS

You can find the distillery near Perth at Newburgh by A913.

PRACTICAL INFORMATION

DISTILLERY / WHISKY BAR
LINDORES ABBEY DISTILLERY
Abbey Road,
Newburgh
Fife, KY14 6HH
+44 (0) 1337 842547
info@lindoresabbeydistillery.com
www.lindoresabbey.com

RESTAURANT / CAFÉ
EAST PORT GARAGE AND COFFEE SHOP
Cupar Road,
Newburgh
Fife, KY14 6HA
+44 (0) 1337 840379
*https://www.facebook.com/eastportgara-
geandcoffeeshop*

MORE INFORMATION ABOUT THE AREA
KINGDOM HOUSE
Kingdom Avenue,
Glenrothes
Fife, KY7 5LT
+44 (0) 3451 555555
promoting.fife@fife.gov.uk
www.welcometofife.com

ACCOMMODATION OPTION
SYKES COTTAGES LTD
Head office: One City Place,
Chester
Cheshire, CH1 3BQ
+44 (0) 1244 356666
info@sykescottages.co.uk
www.sykescottages.co.uk

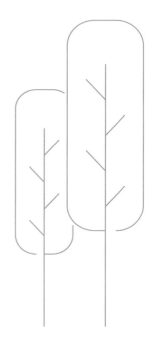

BRACKLINN FALLS

BEAUTIFUL WATERFALLS AND A WEE BIT OF HILL WALKING.

▷ START AND END POINT	✕ DESTINATION
PARKING LOT AT BRACKLINN FALLS	**BRACKLINN FALLS**

◇ WHISKY	⌘ DIFFICULTY
DEANSTON ORGANIC 2001	**WALKING**

☆ HIGHLIGHTS	☉ DURATION OF THE HIKE
BRACKLINN FALLS & BRIDGE, FOREST	**1.5 HOURS 3.3 MILES** (5.4KM)
	⋀ ELEVATION GAIN
	606 FEET (185M)

SINGLE MALT

ALCOHOL **55.5 %** CONTENT

DEANSTON
HIGHLAND SINGLE MALT
SCOTCH WHISKY

👁 **GOLDEN HUES**

👃 **FRUIT, OAK**

👅 **SPICES, HONEY, VANILLA**

🛢 **ORGANIC FINO FINISH**

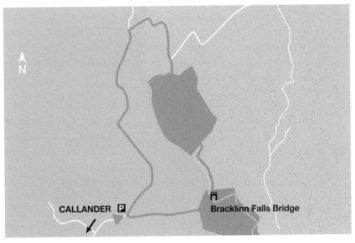

CALLANDER 🅿

Bracklinn Falls Bridge

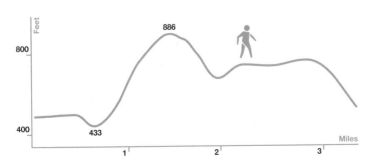

DESCRIPTION OF THE WALK

Bracklinn Falls is in the woods above the town of Callander. Callander is a popular area for both tourists as well as locals. It might be a bit crowded on weekends and holidays around the waterfall, but as soon as you begin to climb the steep path up the hill it will become more quiet, as this path is not suitable for people with baby buggies or people with walking difficulties. Most people just come to see the waterfalls. But with just a bit of effort (and sweat) you get to experience the true beauty of nature, so climb that hill!

In order to combine this amazing walk with the distillery you have to drive a bit, but not much, and trust me, it is worth it. The waterfalls alone are beautiful enough to tempt anyone to come here, but the real pièce de résistance is the moment you exit the woods and come face to face with an amazing view of the mountains, and the river running below. If you don't lose your breath hiking up the path towards the forest, you definitely will when you lay eyes on the view.

You don't have to bring your own lunch as the distillery has a café, but if the weather is nice and you have the time, I would recommend that you have a picnic.

The route is simple: follow the signs to the waterfalls, then head up to the forest and then down and back to the parking lot. It is almost impossible to get lost. I get lost easily, but this trip never left me questioning where I had to go, it just left me breathless.

=========================== **TIP** ===========================

It is so very tempting to do chocolate tastings whenever it is possible; trust me, I understand that completely. But if you only do one tour at Deanston, I suggest you try the warehouse experience. It is simply the best.

TURN BY TURN DIRECTIONS

Start from the parking lot at Bracklinn Falls.

1. Take a left at the sign towards the waterfalls. Follow the path.
2. At 0.45 miles turn left up the path and follow it around to the right to reach the waterfalls.
3. This is a great place for a lunch break.
4. Cross the bridge and take a left up the path and keep walking up the hill following the path.
5. At 1.01 miles you reach the forest road. Keep following it through the forest.
6. At 1.57 miles you exit the forest; this is also an excellent place for a lunch break.
    Continue on the road downwards towards the river.
7. At 1.94 miles you reach the bridge crossing the river.
8. Continue walking towards the road and then take a left at 2.07 miles.
9. Follow this road all the way back to the parking lot where you arrive at 3.34 miles.

DEANSTON DISTILLERY

Deanston Distillery is one of the more touristy distilleries (but nothing like the really big distilleries, don't worry). This is partly because it produces marvellous whisky, but also because of the area it is situated in. There is great nature, great walks, gorgeous waterfalls, and plenty of accommodation options nearby. But do not be scared off by the amount of tourists; once your tour starts you will think of nothing but the whisky.

With local ingredients starting from water from the River Teith, running right outside their doorstep, they produce both a core range of whiskies as well as exclusive and limited whiskies. If you go on their 'warehouse 4 experience' tour you get a tour of the distillery as well as a tasting in their warehouse of three of their whiskies straight from the casks. If any of the whiskies catch your fancy you can buy a bottle, fill it, and label it yourself: a unique experience. They are open 7 days a week, and you can book a tour online or on-site. Children are allowed on the tours, but not on the warehouse experience. If in doubt just give the distillery a call, they are very friendly.

There is a café at the distillery that makes delicious food, so there is no need to bring your own lunch on this trip, unless you feel like a picnic. They have a shop as well; it is filled to the brim with delicious whiskies, gifts, and books. If you, like me, prefer a tour without too many tourists, try booking a tour early in the morning or late in the afternoon – that should do the trick.

DRIVING DIRECTIONS

From the car park at Bracklinn Falls drive down to the main street in Callander and head towards A84 Doune. Once you cross the River Teith turn right at B8032 then right again and follow the river for 500 meters and you can see the distillery.

PRACTICAL INFORMATION

DISTILLERY / WHISKY BAR
DEANSTON DISTILLERY
Near Doune, FK16 6AG
+44 (0) 1786 843010
www.deanstonmalt.com

RESTAURANT / CAFÉ
The distillery has a café.

MORE INFORMATION ABOUT THE AREA
INFORMATION AND HERITAGE CENTRE
61–63 Balkerach Street
Doune, FK16 6DF
+44 (0) 1786 841250
info@doune.co
www.doune.co

ACCOMMODATION OPTION
SYKES COTTAGES LTD
Head office: One City Place,
Chester
Cheshire, CH1 3BQ
+44 (0) 1244 356666
info@sykescottages.co.uk
www.sykescottages.co.uk

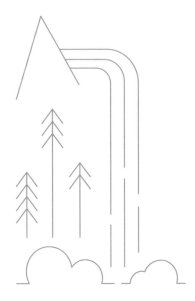

DUN NA CUAICHE

A STEEP WALK, A FAIRY-TALE WOOD, AND A VIEW ON TOP OF THE HILL THAT IS TO DIE FOR.

▷ START AND END POINT	✕ DESTINATION
FRONT STREET CAR PARK BY THE WATER	**DUN NA CUAICHE**

🏷 WHISKY	🎛 DIFFICULTY
LOCH LOMOND 18 YO	**WALKING**

☆ HIGHLIGHTS	⊙ DURATION OF THE HIKE
INVERARAY CASTLE, FOREST TOWER ON THE HILL (DUN NA CUAICHE)	**1.5 HOURS 4.1 MILES** (6.6KM)
	⋀ ELEVATION GAIN
	803 FEET (245M)

ALCOHOL **46** % CONTENT

SINGLE MALT

	CARAMEL
	FRUIT, OAK, DARK RAISIN
	PEAT, SMOOTH, FRUIT, CARAMEL
	OAK BARREL

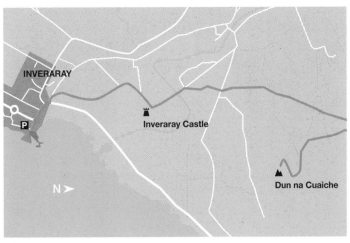

INVERARAY

P

Inveraray Castle

Dun na Cuaiche

N ▶

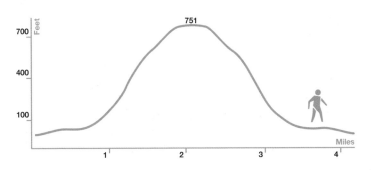

DESCRIPTION OF THE WALK

Once upon a time a tower was built on the top of a hill in Inveraray. Dun na Cuaiche means 'the hill of the cup' and it was built in 1748 purely as a decorative building that is visible from the castle as well as from town. However, the view from the top looking down on the castle and town, as well as that of Loch Fyne and the surrounding hills is even more breath-taking than the one looking up. This is one of those steep walks that you are going to want to do more than once.

Park at the seafront and head towards Inveraray Castle. You don't have to pay an entrance fee to do the walk, but if you would like to visit the castle while you are there, head over to the ticket booth by the castle parking lot. The castle is not open during the winter months but if you happen to visit when it is open, they have a great little café where you can get some lunch, coffee, and cake.

Castle aside, continue up to the forest on the other side of the bridge and head up the blue arrow trail. The path is marked all the way and is very easy to follow.

The forest is stunning, just like a fairy-tale forest, and it has several breath-taking viewpoints during the walk, so keep your camera at hand.

After about 40 to 50 minutes of steep but easy walking you will reach the top. When I was there, I wanted to stay forever because it is so gorgeous. It does get cold during the night, though, so when you are done, head back down the same way you came and get ready for some glorious whisky at The George Hotel, which is just down the road from where you start and end the walk.

TIP

If you have time to spare and would like a bit of history, the prison dating back to the 1820s is right next to The George Hotel. You can find more information on *www.inverarayjail.co.uk*

TURN BY TURN DIRECTIONS

Start from the Front Street car park.

1. Walk along the seafront towards the castle.
2. At 0.13 miles cross the road and walk up to the castle.
3. At 0.62 miles you reach a hedge; take a left and walk towards the woods across the bridge.
4. At 0.76 miles walk up to the right following the blue arrow.
5. At 0.92 miles you reach an open area; cross it and walk into the woods and follow the path to the left. From here on there is only one path up, highlighted all the way with blue arrows.
6. At 2.05 miles you have reached the top.
7. To get back, head down the same way you came and at 4.11 miles you are back at the car park.

THE GEORGE HOTEL AND THE WHISKY BOARD

At the centre of town, you will find The George Hotel. They have lovely rooms, a conservatory, a cocktail bar, a public bar, but – best of all – they have a whisky board tasting!

The George Hotel dates to 1770 and has loads of charisma. It is always busy, so make sure to book a table in advance if you want to eat here. You can do the whisky board tasting in the bar or in the restaurant. They have about 100 different malt whiskies and the whisky board changes with the season. While I visited, they had a "Tour of Scotland" board, and an "Islay Selection". If you are doing the tasting just before dinner, you can choose to order the whisky board with only 15ml of whisky in each glass, but if you want to go all in there is also the option for a 25ml glass. The tasting comes on a wooden board and is presented so you know which is which. This form of presentation for a tasting is absolutely genius. You get to taste 6 different whiskies, and you can savour them one at a time or switch back and forth to compare. And if you don't have to drive, you can always come back and try more whiskies...

DRIVING DIRECTIONS

You can find Inveraray on A83 west from Loch Lomond. The George Hotel is on the main street next to the old Inveraray Jail, you cannot miss it.

PRACTICAL INFORMATION

DISTILLERY / WHISKY BAR
THE GEORGE HOTEL
Main St. East,
Inveraray
Argyll, PA32 8TT
+44 (0) 1499 302111
info@thegeorgehotel.co.uk
www.thegeorgehotel.co.uk

RESTAURANT / CAFÉ
INVERARAY CASTLE
Inveraray
Argyll, PA32 8XE
+44 (0) 1499 302203
enquiries@inveraray-castle.com
www.inveraray-castle.com

MORE INFORMATION ABOUT THE AREA
INVERARAY TOURIST INFORMATION CENTRE
Front Street,
Inveraray
Argyll, PA32 8UY
+44 (0) 8707 200616
info@inveraray.visitscotland.com
www.wtotravel.com

ACCOMMODATION OPTION
THE GEORGE HOTEL
(see information above)

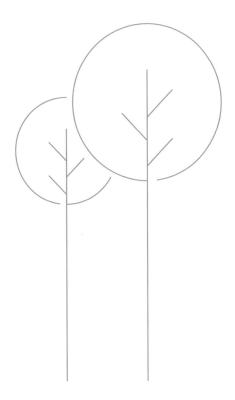

BLACKNESS

EASY WALK WITH STUNNING VIEWS AND A CASTLE AT THE END, WHAT MORE CAN ONE ASK FOR?

▷ START AND END POINT

CARRIDEN WATER PLANT

✕ DESTINATION

CASTLE BLACKNESS

◈ WHISKY

CHAMPANY HIGHLAND SINGLE MALT SCOTCH WHISKY

▦ DIFFICULTY

WALKING

☆ HIGHLIGHTS

THE FORTH BRIDGES, BLACKNESS CASTLE

⊙ DURATION OF THE HIKE

2 HOURS 5.3 MILES (8.5KM)

𝗔 ELEVATION GAIN

443 FEET (135M)

SINGLE MALT

ALCOHOL **40 %** CONTENT

Highland
Single Malt
Scotch Whisky

CARAMEL

FRUIT, SPICES

OAK, FRUIT, SPICES

A SECRET

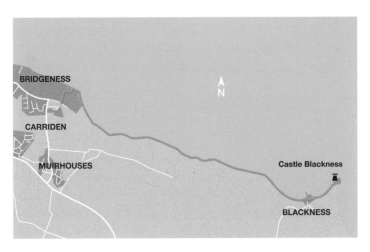

BRIDGENESS

CARRIDEN

MUIRHOUSES

Castle Blackness

BLACKNESS

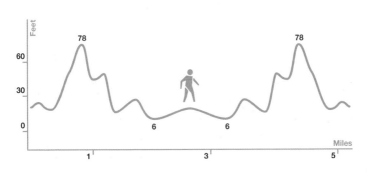

Feet

78

78

60

30

0

6

6

Miles

1

3

5

DESCRIPTION OF THE WALK

If you only have a few days at your disposal in Scotland, this is the perfect place to go. Close enough to Edinburgh Airport for you to swish back and forth within an hour and far enough away to reward you with stunning views and the quietness of the countryside.

It is possible to walk from the Champany Inn to the start point of the walk, but the road is just not made for walking, or bicycling for that matter, so grab your car and head to the starting point: the waste water plant facility. There is no parking lot, but it is possible to park along the residential area for however long you need.

When you are ready, head left after the water plant and follow the turn-by-turn directions. After a short walk you can see the beautiful Forth Bridges on the horizon – old and new structures blending and complementing each other and the nature surrounding them. When you near Blackness you can see the castle from afar, looming in the distance.

I recommend visiting the castle as it is gorgeous and offers lots of historical insight and great views.

If you get hungry on the way there is a little pub called The Lobster Pot on the main road in Blackness; it is very colourful so you can't miss it. They serve great food, and the staff is very friendly.

Head back the same way you came and find your way to The Champany Inn.

DID YOU KNOW?

Sometimes you will come across a bottle of single malt whisky that does not reveal which distiller it is from. It is a secret, but if you know your whisky you might be able to guess. The Champany whisky is one of those bottles. Give it a try and see if you can guess where it is from…

TURN BY TURN DIRECTIONS

Start from the parking close to the waste water plant.

1. To your left just after the water plant there is a road; head down that way.
2. At 0.09 miles take the right path.
3. Within minutes of walking along the smaller path, you can view the bridges in the distance.
4. Follow the path all the way up to the woodland area and continue on the path to Blackness. You can't go wrong.
5. At 2.27 miles you have reached the small town of Blackness. Continue through the town with the coast on your left all the way up to the castle.
6. Head back the same way.
7. You arrive back at 5.28 miles.

CHAMPANY INN

Only a 20-minute drive away from Edinburgh, Champany Inn is the perfect little getaway. It offers charming ambiance, lovely rooms, delightful staff, and food and drink to die for. There is a restaurant, a chop house, and a bar at the inn, everything you need after a long day of walking. If you feel like dressing up, you can book a table at the restaurant, and if you are in the mood for something more casual, you can dine at the chop house. The inn really does have everything your heart desires, even an extensive wine cellar.

And even better is the bar, where the friendly and knowledgeable staff is ready to guide you through a whisky tasting of your choice. It is a popular place so it is best to book in advance, and if you have any questions, they are always happy to help.

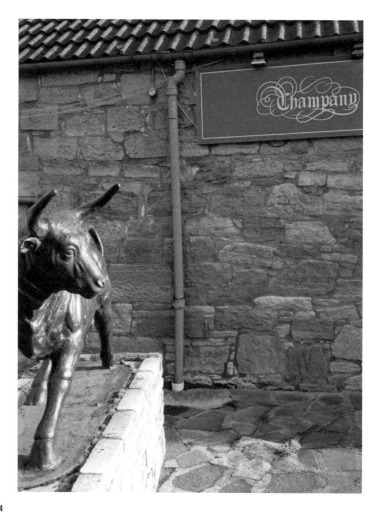

DRIVING DIRECTIONS

Carriden is right next to Bo'ness off the A993. From Carriden, take the M9 and leave it at A803 towards Bo'ness. Champany Inn is situated on the road.

PRACTICAL INFORMATION

DISTILLERY / WHISKY BAR
THE CHAMPANY INN
Linlithgow
West Lothian, EH49 7LU
+44 (0) 1506 834532
reception@champany.com
www.champany.com

RESTAURANT / CAFÉ
THE LOBSTER POT
18 The Square,
Blackness
Falkirk, EH49 7NL
+44 (0) 1506 830086
info@lobster-pot.co.uk
www.lobster-pot.co.uk

MORE INFORMATION ABOUT THE AREA
www.linlithgow.info

ACCOMMODATION OPTION
THE CHAMPANY INN
(see information above)

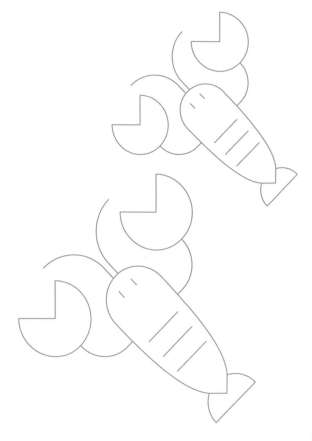

LOCH TAY

POSSIBLY THE MOST BEAUTIFUL WALK IN ALL OF SCOTLAND,
BUT ALSO THE MOST WET AND MUDDY WALK. BE WARNED.

▷ START AND END POINT

THE FALLS OF DOCHART INN

✕ DESTINATION

LOCH TAY

🏷 WHISKY

LEDAIG
10 YO

🔡 DIFFICULTY

WALKING

☆ HIGHLIGHTS

**BIRD WATCHING,
THE OLD BRIDGE,
DOCHART VIADUCT,
THE WATERFALL
BRIDGE IN TOWN**

🕙 DURATION OF THE HIKE

1.5 HOURS
3.3 MILES (5.3KM)

⌂ ELEVATION GAIN

240 FEET
(73M)

ALCOHOL
46.3 %
CONTENT

SINGLE MALT

1798
LEDAIG

👁	LIGHT GOLD
👃	SMOKE, PEAT, SPICE
👅	PEAT, CHOCOLATE, SPICE
🛢	BOURBON CASK

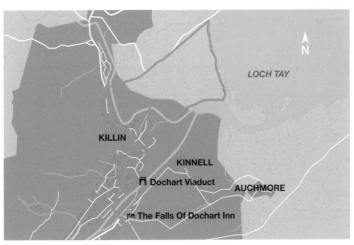

LOCH TAY

KILLIN

KINNELL

Ⅱ Dochart Viaduct

AUCHMORE

The Falls Of Dochart Inn

N

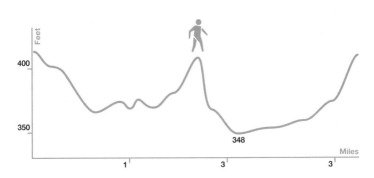

Feet

400

350

348

Miles

1   3   3

DESCRIPTION OF THE WALK

If you are feeling adventurous, you can undertake this walk during the wet season. If you are not Scottish, I can already hear you thinking, "Is there ever a non-wet season?" To that I can only say that summertime is the best time to do this.

I suggest you bring waders or even swimming trunks! If you do decide to venture out on this walk you will be greatly rewarded with splendid views of the mountains and the lush area of Killin and Loch Tay.

Head out from The Falls Of Dochart Inn and bring a lunch pack made by the chef from the inn with you. Make sure to ask for a dram to be packed into it. I chose the Ledaig with just the right amount of peat and smoke for such a cold and wet walk, but they have plenty of whiskies to choose from. Follow the turn-by-turn directions and enjoy the glorious scenery of Loch Tay as you walk along it. If you are lucky you might spot some interesting and rare birds.

Along the way you cross an old bridge and a viaduct bridge with spectacular photo opportunities. It is also a great spot to enjoy a bit of whisky. If you are a bit of a photo nerd (or married to one, like I am) you can spend a lot of time on this walk taking pictures. But that's all part of creating treasured memories.

When you reach the town of Killin, make sure you stop and admire the Dochart Falls; they are truly stunning to behold.

TIP

If you are interested in birds, bring your binoculars with you on this walk as there are many different birds to see in the area.

TURN BY TURN DIRECTIONS

1. Head out from The Falls of Dochart Inn and cross the bridge towards town.
2. Follow the Main St. through town. At 0.86 miles turn right at Pier Rd and cross the bridge.
3. At 1.06 miles you will reach Killin Cemetery and a forest. Go into the forest and follow the path straight ahead.
4. At 1.26 miles go to the right and follow the path along the road.
5. At 1.6 miles you reach a gate on your right; walk through it and continue the path along Loch Tay.
6. At 4.12 km / 2.56 miles you arrive at a wooden gate. Walk through it and head left over the old bridge. Follow the walking path from here.
7. At 2.81 miles you reach Lion Rd. Walk down this road.
8. At 2.82 miles walk left onto the path and continue along it.
9. At 2.98 miles you reach the Viaduct. Continue ahead.
10. At 3.08 miles you reach a gravel road, follow this road and at 3.28 miles you arrive back at your starting point.

THE FALLS OF DOCHART INN

Your starting point in this chapter is the same as in the next, the charming Falls of Dochart Inn. You will be out and about in the ever changing Scottish weather, so make sure to gear up. There are several places during the walk that can serve as a perfect picnic spot. The river runs all the way through Killin. The Falls of Dochart can even be admired on the village bridge just outside the Falls of Dochart Inn. If the weather is sunny you can enjoy your lunch there. But my advice is to order a lunch pack with whisky from the Inn (have your own small tasting bottles ready in case the Inn doesn't have any) and set out on your adventure.

DRIVING DIRECTIONS

You find the town of Killin on the A827 off the A85.

PRACTICAL INFORMATION

DISTILLERY / WHISKY BAR
THE FALLS OF DOCHART INN
Gray Street
Killin, FK21 8SL
+44 (0)1567 820270
info@fallsofdochartinn.co.uk
www.fallsofdochartinn.co.uk

RESTAURANT / CAFÉ
Bring a picnic.

MORE INFORMATION ABOUT THE AREA
www.killin.net

ACCOMMODATION OPTION
THE FALLS OF DOCHART INN
(see information above)

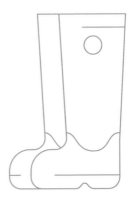

SRON A' CHLACHAIN

A STEEP WALK WITH A GLORIOUS VIEW OF LOCH TAY AND THE TOWN OF KILLIN.

▷ START AND END POINT	✕ DESTINATION
THE FALLS OF DOCHART INN	**SRON A' CHLACHAIN**

🍾 WHISKY	⌘ DIFFICULTY
ABERLOUR 12 YO	**HIKING**

☆ HIGHLIGHTS	⏱ DURATION OF THE HIKE
THE WATERFALL BRIDGE IN TOWN, THE TOP OF SRON A' CLACHAIN	**1.5 HOURS 3.1 MILES** (5KM)
	⋀ ELEVATION GAIN
	1365 FEET (416M)

SINGLE MALT

ALCOHOL **40 %** CONTENT

GOLDEN AMBER

FRUIT, SPICES

PEAT, SMOOTH, FRUIT, CARAMEL

DOUBLE CASK: OAK AND SHERRY

ABERLOUR
ESTD 1879
DOUBLE CASK MATURED
12
YEARS OLD

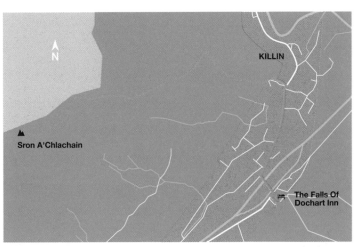

KILLIN

Sron A'Chlachain

The Falls Of Dochart Inn

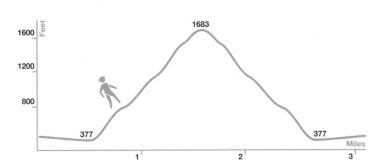

DESCRIPTION OF THE WALK

Fancy a wee hill walk? Look no further, this is a perfect little walk that takes you high above the town of Killin.

Set out from the Falls of Dochart Inn and cross the bridge towards town. When you get to the park, simply head through it and walk up the hill towards the woods. Once in the woods it's easy to follow the path, though you might get out of breath a bit as it's steep at times. Walk up and up and up until you finally reach the top. There might be sheep grazing during milder months, but they are friendly enough.

The view all the way up is spectacular so if you need a break to catch your breath, photography is the perfect excuse: Just snap away.

Once on top you have the whole of Killin and Loch Tay at your feet; it's an amazing vista best experienced on days with clear skies.

Head down the same way and walk back to the inn for a well-deserved dram of whisky.

TIP

Make sure to stop by Shutters Restaurant & Café as they have the best cappuccino in town. Incidentally, this walk passes the café twice. Quite by accident of course...

TURN BY TURN DIRECTIONS

Start from the inn parking.

1. Go ahead across the waterfall bridge towards the centre of town.
2. At 0.43 miles you reach Shutters Restaurant & Café. Go left towards the park and follow the path straight ahead.
3. At 0.52 miles you reach a sign that says "Sron a' Chlachain". Follow that sign walking up the hill towards the forest.
4. At 0.68 miles you reach a wooden ladder which will take you across a fence and into the forest. From here on you can't really go wrong. Just head up.
5. At 1.54 miles you have reached the top.
6. Head down and walk back the same way you came.
7. At 3.07 miles you are back at the inn.

THE FALLS OF DOCHART INN

A charming old blacksmith's shop from the 18th century makes for the perfect whisky stop while in the small town of Killin. When you enter the bar, you are greeted by an open fire, friendly staff, and a well-stocked whisky bar. It does tend to get busy so make sure to book in advance if you want a table. If you haven't phoned ahead the friendly staff will try their best to seat you. The inn is the perfect place to stay if you want to spend several days walking in the area and it is situated in a romantic setting. It is right across from the beautiful waterfalls of Dochart. I can highly recommend having dinner here and pairing a dram of whisky with their hot and cold whisky-smoked salmon, it is delicious. Whisky is brilliant, but whisky paired with food is the absolute best.

DRIVING DIRECTIONS

You find the town of Killin by driving off the A85 onto the A827 and Dochart Road. The Falls of Dochart Inn is on Gray Street.

PRACTICAL INFORMATION

DISTILLERY / WHISKY BAR
THE FALLS OF DOCHART INN
Gray Street
Killin, FK21 8SL
+44 (0) 1567 820270
info@fallsofdochartinn.co.uk
www.fallsofdochartinn.co.uk

RESTAURANT / CAFÉ
THE FALLS OF DOCHART INN
(see information above)

MORE INFORMATION ABOUT THE AREA
www.trossachs.co.uk/regions/killin/

ACCOMMODATION OPTION
THE FALLS OF DOCHART INN
(see information above)

GLEN OGLE RAILWAY

THIS IS A CHALLENGING HIKE FULL OF ADVENTURE.

▷ START AND END POINT

AUCHRAW TERRACE

✕ DESTINATION

GLEN OGLE RAILWAY BRIDGE

🍶 WHISKY

SCALLYWAG BLENDED MALT

▦ DIFFICULTY

HIKING

☆ HIGHLIGHTS

THE VIADUCT, MILITARY ROAD

☉ DURATION OF THE HIKE

3 HOURS
6.5 MILES (10.5KM)

△ ELEVATION GAIN

715 FEET
(218M)

BLENDED MALT

ALCOHOL **46** % CONTENT

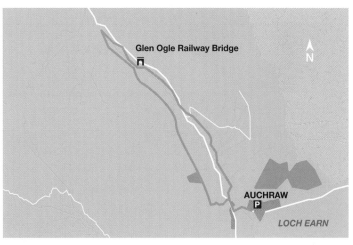

👁	GOLDEN
👃	VANILLA, OAK, CHRISTMAS CAKE
👅	OAK, VANILLA, SMOOTH SHERRY
🛢	SHERRY AND BOURBON CASKS

Glen Ogle Railway Bridge

N

AUCHRAW
P

LOCH EARN

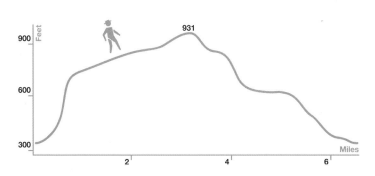

931

DESCRIPTION OF THE WALK

Be advised that the locals do not recommend this walk during wintertime, fall, or any rainy seasons or periods. There is another, easier way to get to the railway path and back again if necessary, but where would be the fun in that? Get ready for an adventure that will make you feel like a mountain goat (I mean that in the best sense). This is a long, strenuous, and probably wet walk, especially on the second half of the tour. You are pretty much walking along the path of sheep and goats so channel your inner mountain goat and start walking!

You start off at the public parking lot and head up to the main road and up towards the woodland area. It is a bit steep and can be very muddy and slippery if it is raining or has been raining before: Be careful. At the top of the hill you reach the railway road and from here it is easy and peaceful walking. Enjoy it while it lasts...

The railway bridge is gorgeous to look at, and you can easily spend a lot of time there just taking photographs.

When you reach a small waterfall on your left it is time to take a right and head down, following the directions. There is a path, it is just not always visible so you have to follow the GPX file as weather may have changed the accessibility of the path. You might even have to make your own path to find your way. It is all part of the adventure!

Once you make your way through trees and ferns and get to the road, cross it and go through a gate. Now starts the second half of the walk: the way back. You can't really get lost on this last bit, but it is straining for the ankles to walk it as you will mostly be walking on the side of a hill. Follow the GPX file and the occasional signposts, and eventually, after several jumps over rivers running downhill and ferns the height of a person, you reach a field with a bridge. Cross it and head towards the road, and before you know it you will be back to where you started. After this trip, you most certainly deserve a glass of whisky. Make that a double!

=============== **DID YOU KNOW?** ===============

The marvellous path which can be seen from the new road below the viaduct was originally built as a military road used by the British army in their quest to quell the last of the Jacobites in the highlands.

TURN BY TURN DIRECTIONS

Start from the parking lot on Auchraw Terrace.

1. Walk to the right up to the main road. At 0.28 miles go right and walk along the road.
2. At 0.44 miles cross the road, head up, and take the path to the right.
3. Follow the path up the hill and at 0.71 miles you reach the top where the railway trail is. Go right.
4. At 2.42 miles you reach the iconic bridge.
5. At 3.27 miles go right and up over the fence. Follow path down.
6. Follow the path and signposts and at 4.66 miles you will reach the road.
   Cross it and walk 0.02 miles until you reach a path to the left. Go left.
7. Follow the path and signposts and at 5.97 miles cross the small bridge and
   head towards the gate at the left.
8. Walk to and through the gate by the road.
9. Walk left towards town.
10. At 6.23 miles turn left and walk to the parking lot.
11. At 6.51 miles you arrive at the parking lot.

THE CLACHAN COTTAGE HOTEL

Right beside Loch Earn you find the idyllic Clachan Cottage Hotel, perfect for holiday breaks, dining, and, more importantly, whisky tasting! Enter at the bar and find a table by the window that overlooks the loch. There are many whiskies to choose from and the owner, Alan Garnier, is more than happy to help you decide which one to taste. While you are tasting whisky or waiting for a well-deserved dinner after your long walk, ask Alan about the history of the area; he is an absolute gem and a source of local knowledge.

If you visit here during summer the hotel has a lovely area outside where you can sit.

Clachan Cottage Hotel has plenty of rooms if you want a base from where you can set off walking. There is a plethora of walks in the area, enough to keep you busy for quite some time.

Make sure you are well rested for this walk. Keep your spirits high, you are in for a tough one.

DRIVING DIRECTIONS

From the parking lot, drive left and further down the road where you can find The Clachan Cottage Hotel.

PRACTICAL INFORMATION

DISTILLERY / WHISKY BAR
CLACHAN COTTAGE HOTEL
Lochside, Lochearnhead
Stirling, FK
19 8PU
+44 (0) 2080 898579
info@clachancottagehotel.co.uk
www.clachancottagehotel.co.uk

RESTAURANT / CAFÉ
CLACHAN COTTAGE HOTEL
(see information above)

MORE INFORMATION ABOUT THE AREA
www.gateway-to-the-scottish-highlands.com

ACCOMMODATION OPTION
CLACHAN COTTAGE HOTEL
(see information above)

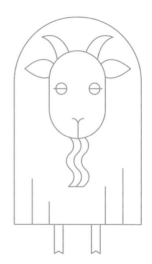

DUNSTAFFNAGE CASTLE

A PERFECT LITTLE WALK FULL OF NATURE, HISTORY, AND FUN.

▷ START AND END POINT	✕ DESTINATION
CASTLE PARKING LOT	**CASTLE GROUNDS AND FOREST**

◈ WHISKY	▦ DIFFICULTY
THE GLENROTHES SELECT RESERVE	**WALKING**

☆ HIGHLIGHTS	◷ DURATION OF THE HIKE
CASTLE DUNSTAFFNAGE, THE CHAPEL IN THE WOODS, THE BEACH	**0.75 HOUR 1.7 MILES** (2.8KM)
	△ ELEVATION GAIN
	135 FEET (41M)

SINGLE MALT

ALCOHOL **43** % CONTENT

THE GLENROTHES
SELECT RESERVE
SPEYSIDE SINGLE MALT SCOTCH WHISKY

GOLDEN

OAK, VANILLA, PLUM

VANILLA, ORANGE, SPICE

N/A

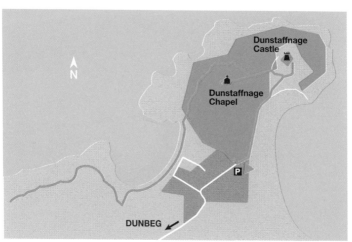

Dunstaffnage Castle

Dunstaffnage Chapel

P

N

DUNBEG

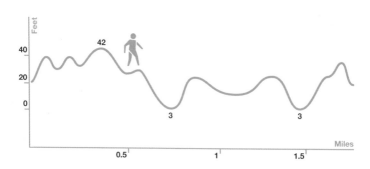

Feet

42

40

20

0

3

3

0.5

1

1.5

Miles

DESCRIPTION OF THE WALK

Not far from Oban you will find Castle Dunstaffnage, built before 1240 as a mighty stronghold of the MacDougalls and conquered by Robert the Bruce in 1308. This castle has seen a lot of prisoners and a lot of fighting. It is one of the oldest standing castles in Scotland and it is fascinating to walk inside a place with this much history. I highly recommend that you visit it while you are there. It is open from the start of April to the end of September.

The chapel lies in the woods and looks like something out of a fantasy or historical novel.

The walk itself is short and fairly easy. The trail can be difficult to spot while you are walking through the woods and you might have to jump over puddles or go underneath low-hanging branches in order to get through, but that's all part of the fun.

If you park at the main parking lot, please note that it closes when the castle closes. But right next to it there is another parking lot where you can park for longer. The walk along the sea is beautiful and you can extend your walk further that way. If you have just returned from a wee bit of mountain walking and need more fun than exercise, you can head straight for the castle.

When you reach the beach, and if the weather is good, you can take advantage of some great photo opportunities there. When you are all done head towards the parking lot, follow the directions, and get ready for some whisky.

===================================== TIP =====================================

If you are a history geek, this is the place to go. Dunstaffnage Castle was built in the early 1200s and besieged by no other than the famous Robert the Bruce in the early 1300s after his victory at the Pass of Brander. As if this was not enough history to seep into the castle walls, Dunstaffnage also played a part in the aftermath of the Jacobite uprising, where a young unlikely heroine helped Bonnie Prince Charlie to flee after the defeat at Culloden. The prince escaped, but the girl, Flora MacDonald, was captured and held captive at Dunstaffnage Castle until she was moved to the Tower of London.

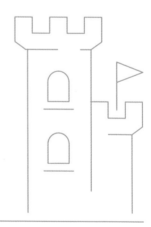

TURN BY TURN DIRECTIONS

Start from the parking lot. (make sure to check when it closes before you head off!)

1. Head towards the castle with the coastline to your right.
2. If you like you can continue onwards along the coast and come back afterward. Otherwise, head up the gravel path to the castle and take a left into the woods.
3. Head up to the castle, it has great views, but mind that you must pay an entrance fee if you want to go inside.
4. From the castle, head towards the woods and enter at 0.28 miles.
5. At 0.35 miles you reach the old chapel in the small forest.
6. Head back and at 0.44 miles take the small wood path to your left.
7. Walk through the woods along the path with the sea on your right.
8. At 0.62 miles choose the right path to get back to walk along the beach in order to take in the stunning sea view.
9. Walk along the beach for as long as you like.
10. Head back to where the path was divided in the woods and take a right.
11. At 1.73 miles you return to the parking lot.

THE LORNE BAR

In the heart of the bustling town of Oban you'll find The Lorne Bar. It is unpretentious, down to earth, and has a wide variety of whiskies. The whiskies are all displayed and encircle the bar area which is based in the middle of the room. The Lorne Bar offers everything you need after a day of hiking: great food, friendly staff, live music at the weekends, and comfortable seating. You are welcome to bring your dog. There is also a lovely beer garden where you can enjoy your whisky in the warm summer months.

=== TIP ===

If you feel like visiting a more touristy distillery, Oban Distillery is not far from the whisky bar. But it is busy, so make sure to book in advance.

DRIVING DIRECTIONS

From the castle, drive back on Kirk Road and take a left on Jane Road and you reach A85. Go right and you get to Oban. In Oban park in the vicinity of Tweedale Street, walk to Stevenson Street, and you arrive at the Lorne Bar.

PRACTICAL INFORMATION

DISTILLERY / WHISKY BAR
THE LORNE
Stevenson Street
Oban, PA34 5NA
+44 (0) 1631 570020
info@thelornebaroban.co.uk
www.thelornebaroban.co.uk

RESTAURANT / CAFÉ
THE LORNE HOTEL
(see information above)

MORE INFORMATION ABOUT THE AREA
www.oban.org.uk

ACCOMMODATION OPTION
SYKES COTTAGES LTD
Head office: One City Place,
Chester
Cheshire, CH1 3BQ
+44 (0) 1244 356666
info@sykescottages.co.uk
www.sykescottages.co.uk

LOCH KATRINE

AN ETHEREAL WALK ALONG THE BEAUTIFUL LAKESIDE AND UP THE HILLS.
A SIMPLY STUNNING TRIP THAT WILL LEAVE YOU SPEECHLESS.

▷ START AND END POINT

LOCH KATRINE PARKING

✕ DESTINATION

LOCH KATRINE AND SURROUNDING HILLS

🏷 WHISKY

GLENGOYNE
12 YO

🔡 DIFFICULTY

WALKING

☆ HIGHLIGHTS

VIEW OF ELLEN'S ISLE, PICNIC AREA, PHOTO OPPORTUNITY

🕐 DURATION OF THE HIKE

3 HOURS
6.7 MILES (11KM)

△ ELEVATION GAIN

1105 FEET
(337M)

SINGLE MALT

43 % ALCOHOL CONTENT	
MEDIUM GOLDEN	
SPICE, VANILLA	
SPICE, MARZIPAN, WALNUT	
SHERRY CASK	

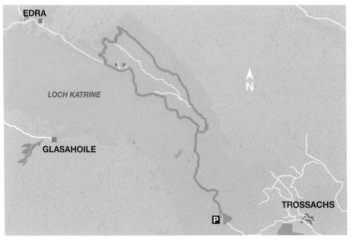

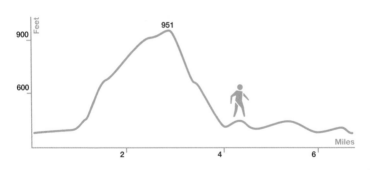

DESCRIPTION OF THE WALK

Prepare to be amazed by nature's beauty on this walk, it is absolutely otherworldly. You start off from the parking area at the Loch Katrine visitor centre and head up the road along the lake. The first thing you see may be the beautiful steamship *Sir Walter Scott*. This walk and the next walk in the book will set off from the same place. If you feel like taking a trip on the boat before you head off it is best done during fair weather, so better take the chance if you have it. I did this walk looking out on the loch, not sailing on it. Sailing I saved for after walking up Ben A'an.

Head past the ships and past the eco-lodges and follow the road until you start walking up the hill. Once up, just follow the path forward and then eventually downhill again. From the top of the hill you get a beautiful view of Loch Katrine and the surrounding mountains. When descending you walk through woodland and then exit onto the main road along the loch. Follow the road back with the water now on your right side, and enjoy the vista. Along the way you come across a clearing that is great for picnics and photo sessions. Continue your walk and you reach the point where you can see Ellen's Isle. This is a small island in Loch Katrine named after a heroic young woman who sought refuge there. Continue on your walk homeward and you reach the parking lot again.

Sir Walter Scott was inspired by Ellen's Isle and her story when he wrote his famous poem "The Lady of the Lake".

TURN BY TURN DIRECTIONS

Start from the parking lot at Loch Katrine.

1. Head down the road with the water on your left.
2. Follow this road along the water until at 1.18 miles you take the path up to the right.
3. At 1.45 miles continue walking straight ahead along the path.
4. At 1.69 miles take the right path and continue upwards.
5. At 3.41 miles go right, walk through the gate, and continue.
6. At 3.97 miles you have reached the main road.
7. Turn left and head back towards the parking lot.
8. At 4.61 miles you pass an open area perfect for a picnic and photo shoot.
9. Continue until, at 6.76 miles, you reach the parking lot.

THE STEAMSHIP CAFÉ

This is probably the most lowkey and surprising choice of place for drinking whisky, but it is perfectly situated right by Loch Katrine. It's warm, it's cosy, and the staff is friendly. If the weather is good, try finding a spot outside; the view overlooking the loch is lovely. They have a decent selection of whisky and serve food, so you don't have to bring lunch on your walk. They are usually open daily, but if you want to make sure that they are open when you get there, just give them a call. They also make food to go, so if you feel like a picnic, just order the food you like and tell them you'd like to take it with you.

If you don't find a whisky you fancy in the café, have a look at the little shop, they have whisky as well. Some of the bottles are small and handy to have in a backpack, and then it's just a question of choosing a beautiful spot among many along your walk to taste a wee dram.

DRIVING DIRECTIONS

If you are travelling via Callander take the A84 to Kilmahog and then the A821 through Brig o'Turk. Set your Sat Nav GPS to N56.233686 W4.428894; just entering the post code into the GPS will guide you to Loch Achray Hotel which is 1.4 miles from your destination. If in doubt give Loch Katrine Cruise, Cycle, Walk & Stay a call and they will help you find your way to the Loch.

PRACTICAL INFORMATION

DISTILLERY / WHISKY BAR
THE STEAMSHIP CAFÉ
Loch Katrine Visitor Centre Trossachs Pier
Loch Katrine
Callander, FK17 8HZ
+44 (0) 1877 376317
enquiries@lochkatrine.com
www.lochkatrine.com

RESTAURANT / CAFÉ
THE STEAMSHIP CAFÉ
(see information above)

MORE INFORMATION ABOUT THE AREA
www.lochkatrine.com

ACCOMMODATION OPTION
LOCH KATRINE
CRUISE, CYCLE, WALK & STAY
Trossachs Pier,
Loch Katrine
Callander, FK17 8HZ
+44 (0) 1877 376315
enquiries@lochkatrine.com
www.lochkatrine.com

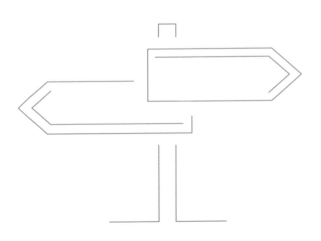

BEN A'AN

CONQUER THE MINIATURE MOUNTAIN AND THEN ALL STEAM AHEAD
WHILE YOU ENJOY YOUR DRAM OF WHISKY.

▷ START AND END POINT

LOCH KATRINE PARKING

✕ DESTINATION

BEN A'AN

◇ WHISKY

BUNNAHABHAIN
12 YO

▦ DIFFICULTY

HIKING

☆ HIGHLIGHTS

TOP OF BEN A'AN, BOAT TRIP ON THE LOCH

◷ DURATION OF THE HIKE

1.5 HOURS
2.3 MILES (3.7KM)

△ ELEVATION GAIN

1115 FEET
(430M)

SINGLE MALT

 GOLDEN

 SWEET, MALT

MALT, SHERRY, SULTANAS

BOURBON CASK
SHERRY CASK

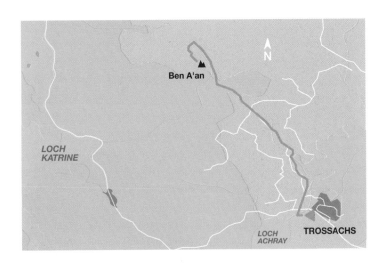

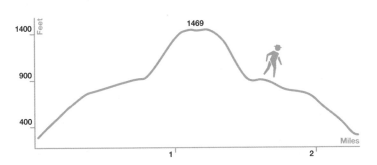

DESCRIPTION OF THE WALK

Start your day by walking up Ben A'an feeling like a great mountaineer and end the day by putting on your imaginary captain's hat shouting "Ship Ahoy" while sailing slowly up the Loch Katrine. Life doesn't get much better than that.

Head off from either the parking lot at Loch Katrine or drive down the road and park at the parking lot by Ben A'an. The Ben A'an parking lot is small and there is not room for a lot of cars. The walk from Loch Katrine to the Ben A'an parking lot is 1.7 km but it is a fairly dull walk.

You can't really go wrong on this walk; there are enough signs, and the path is very well maintained. It is so well maintained that you should be able to walk this walk all year round, but of course if there is a lot of snow it can be difficult to see it, so be careful.

The great maintenance is also the reason why this mountain is so well visited, and you will probably meet a lot of other walkers on your way to the top. Try doing the walk early in the morning if you want to meet fever tourists.

The beautiful Loch Katrine is not just a "pretty loch", it is also a water reservoir for Glasgow and surrounding areas and has been since 1859. Because of danger of polluting the water, oil-fired vessels are now not allowed to sail on the loch. The majestic steamboat *Sir Walter Scott* has been converted to use biodiesel fuel when transporting tourists on board during the summer season. This is in order to keep the water as clean as possible.

TURN BY TURN DIRECTIONS

Start from the Parking lot at the Ben A'an.

1. Cross the road, head up the path.
2. At 0.06 miles walk straight ahead.
3. At 0.60 miles walk straight ahead.
4. At 1.16 miles you reach the top.
5. Head down the same way.
6. At 2.31 miles you reach the parking lot.

LADY OF THE LAKE

I have had whisky on the top of a mountain (or, a large hill in Scottish terms), in a lush meadow, in decadent bars, in stunning distilleries, and in pubs filled to the brim with history and charm, but I have to say that drinking that dram on the *Lady of the Lake* after a long hill walk was an outstanding experience for me.

You can choose between the delightful old steamship *Sir Walter Scott* or the modern MV *Lady of the Lake*. Obviously, the old steamship is the more charming and picturesque ship, but that also makes it the more touristy ship. Hence, I chose the *Lady of the Lake* (to be fair, I also didn't want to wait for the other boat).

Both boats have their charm, but the important thing for this book is that you can have whisky on board. There are not a lot of whiskies to choose from, but they've got some good ones.

DRIVING DIRECTIONS

To get to Loch Katrine set your Sat Nav GPS to N56.233686 W4.428894; just entering the post code on the GPS will guide you to Loch Achray Hotel which is 1.4 miles from your destination. If in doubt give Loch Katrine Cruise, Cycle, Walk & Stay a call and they will help you find your way to the Loch.

The Ben A'an parking lot you find on A821 just a few minutes from Loch Katrine.

PRACTICAL INFORMATION

DISTILLERY / WHISKY BAR
THE STEAMSHIP CAFÉ
Loch Katrine Visitor Centre Trossachs Pier
Loch Katrine
Callander, FK17 8HZ
+44 (0) 1877 376317
enquiries@lochkatrine.com
www.lochkatrine.com

RESTAURANT / CAFÉ
THE STEAMSHIP CAFÉ
(see information above)

MORE INFORMATION ABOUT THE AREA
www.lochkatrine.com

ACCOMMODATION OPTION
LOCH KATRINE
CRUISE, CYCLE, WALK & STAY
Trossachs Pier,
Loch Katrine
Callander, FK17 8HZ
+44 (0) 1877 376315

LUNAN BAY

ENJOY THE DRAMATIC ANGUS COASTLINE AND THE EQUALLY DRAMATIC LOCAL RYE WHISKY.

▷ START AND END POINT

LUNAN FARMS CAMPSITE

✕ DESTINATION

LUNAN BAY

◇ WHISKY

ARBIKIE HIGHLAND RYE

▦ DIFFICULTY

WALKING

☆ HIGHLIGHTS

THE CAVES,
THE BEACH,
RED CASTLE,
DRONE PHOTOGRAPHY
OPPORTUNITY

◴ DURATION OF THE HIKE

1.5 HOURS
3.8 MILES (6.1KM)

⌂ ELEVATION GAIN

413 FEET
(126M)

SINGLE GRAIN SCOTCH WHISKY

ALCOHOL **46 %** CONTENT

CARAMEL GOLDEN

DARK CARAMEL GOLDEN

ORANGE MARMA-LADE, CLOVES, MAPLE SYRUP

CHARRED AMERICAN OAK; ENRICHED IN PEDRO XIMENEZ BARRELS

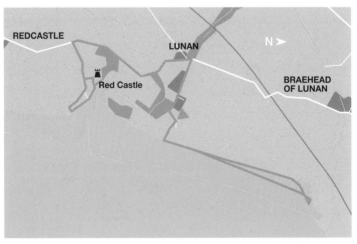

REDCASTLE

LUNAN

N

Red Castle

BRAEHEAD OF LUNAN

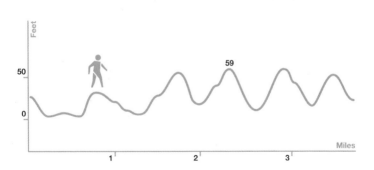

DESCRIPTION OF THE WALK

Is there anything better than a beautiful stroll along the beach, enjoying miles and miles of sand and blue water? Well, perhaps a stroll followed by the best rye whisky in Scotland is better.

Park your car at the parking area by the beach. If the weather permits it, you can go for a dip along your walk; the water is absolutely gorgeous. At the end of the beach you can find a cave, but be careful only to visit it if the tide allows it.

When you walk back you can stop by Lunan House for lunch and coffee, before heading onwards towards the Red Castle and the bird hide.

Follow the turn-by-turn directions and before you know it you are standing on the hill beside the Red Castle, now a ruin, looking out onto the bay. Originally built as a defence against the Vikings, it now lies dormant, a beautiful ruin with a drop-dead gorgeous view that couldn't keep this Danish Viking "at bay". Find your way to the green bird hide. It's not very large but it does the trick if you have the patience for birdwatching. Follow the turn-by-turn directions and head back to the car park and onwards to the Arbikie distillery.

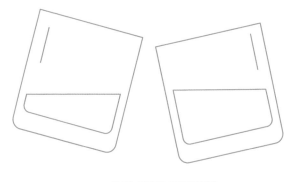

Whisky is a spirit made by distilling fermented cereals. Barley is most used in Scotland.

TURN BY TURN DIRECTIONS

Start at the Lunan Farms Campsite car park.

1. Walk towards the beach and the viewing platform.
2. By the beach walk left and walk along the shore.
3. At 0.68 miles you will reach the cliffs. If the tide is low you can enter the cave.
   After finishing your sightseeing, head back the same way.
4. At 1.49 miles you reach the parking lot again. Walk onwards down the road.
5. At 1.74 miles go left at the big road.
6. At 2.30 miles walk left down towards Red Castle.
7. At 2.45 miles go left up a small path.
8. At 2.49 miles you reach the castle ruins.
9. Walk right down towards the beach.
10. At 2.55 miles walk right along the beach.
11. At 2.67 miles walk up towards the bird hide.
12. At 2.78 miles you reach the bird hide. Turn right and walk towards the road.
13. At 2.98 miles you reach the road. Walk left towards the big road.
14. At 3.54 miles you reach the big road. Turn right.
15. At 3.54 miles turn right towards the parking lot.
16. At 3.79 miles you arrive where you started.

ARBIKIE DISTILLERY

There is a saying in Danish when one gives it their all. The task requires *blod, sved og tårer*, 'blood, sweat, and tears'. The Arbikie Distillery plans on opening their visitor centre very soon. When I visited the site, the foundation was laid but the untrained eye wouldn't have been able to see it for what it really was – a dream coming true. A dream coming true with blood, sweat, and tears. The Stirling family has worked hard to make their dream happen. Together with their brilliant master distiller Kirsty Black and the rest of the brilliant team they have made this estate possible. It is an exciting time for them and for us who get to visit and share that dream. You will know exactly what kind of whisky you are drinking and where it came from, something that most distilleries can't boast about, seeing as Arbikie sows, grows, and harvests their own crops. Furthermore, the Arbikie Highland Rye Single Grain Scots Whisky is the first Scottish Rye in Scotland in over 100 years; that is definitely something that Team Arbikie can be proud of. I can't wait to visit them again and see the dream come true.

DRIVING DIRECTIONS

The Lunan Bay is by the A92 from Arbroath towards Montrose.
The distillery is back on the A92 and up the road on the left. If you set
your Sat Nav to the postal code DD11 4UZ you can find it easily.

PRACTICAL INFORMATION

DISTILLERY / WHISKY BAR
ARBIKIE HIGHLAND ESTATE DISTILLERY
Inverkeilor,
Arbroath
Angus, DD11 4UZ
+44 (0) 1241 830770
info@arbikie.com
www.arbikie.com
www.highlandryewhisky.com

RESTAURANT / CAFÉ
LUNAN HOUSE BAR & DINING ROOM
Lunan Bay,
Arbroath
Angus, DD11 5ST
+44 (0) 1241 830798
bookings@lunanbaystays.scot
www.facebook.com/lunanbaystays

MORE INFORMATION ABOUT THE AREA
www.visitangus.com

ACCOMMODATION OPTION
LUNAN LEISURE LTD
LUNAN FARM
LUNAN BAY
Arbroath
Angus, DD11 5ST
+44 (0) 1241 830334
mail@lunanfarms.co.uk
www.facebook.com/lunanbaystays

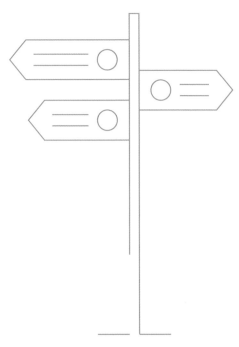

THE CATERTHUNS

SOMETIMES YOU DON'T HAVE TO WANDER FAR AND WIDE TO FIND THE PERFECT SPOT.

▷ START AND END POINT

PARKING AT CATERTHUNS

✕ DESTINATION

THE TWO CATERTHUNS

🏷 WHISKY

GLENCADAM
10 YO

🎴 DIFFICULTY

WALKING

☆ HIGHLIGHTS

THE WHITE & THE BROWN CATERTHUNS

🕙 DURATION OF THE HIKE

1 HOUR
1.9 MILES (3KM)

⌃ ELEVATION GAIN

259 FEET
(79M)

ALCOHOL
46 %
CONTENT

SINGLE MALT

👁	GOLD
👃	SPICE, CITRUS FRUITS, OAK
👄	SPICE, OAK, CITRUS
🛢	BOURBON CASK

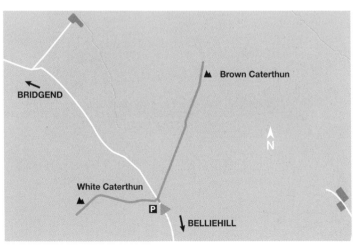

BRIDGEND

Brown Caterthun

N

White Caterthun

P

BELLIEHILL

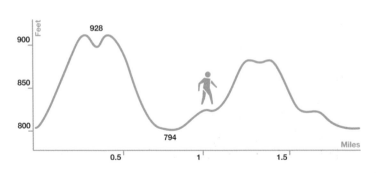

Feet

928

900

850

794

800

0.5   1   1.5

Miles

DESCRIPTION OF THE WALK

This might just be one of the shortest walks in this book. Sometimes there aren't any majestic mountains or flowery meadows on the doorstep of a distillery, but that doesn't mean that you can't have an enjoyable walk with an amazing view and loads of history. And this walk is full of both.

The White and Brown Caterthuns are over 2000 years old and offer a great view over Strathmore and the Angus Glens. On top of each of them you will find remains of a fort, which must have looked very impressive when they were newly built. No one knows exactly what they were built for but that doesn't make them any less impressive.

It is the perfect place to have a picnic; simply decide whether to go left or right first, and then head up the first hill. Seeing as the distillery doesn't have a visitor centre with a café, make sure to bring some food with you.

If you wish to do a more challenging walk, try heading up the eastern parts of the Grampian mountains.

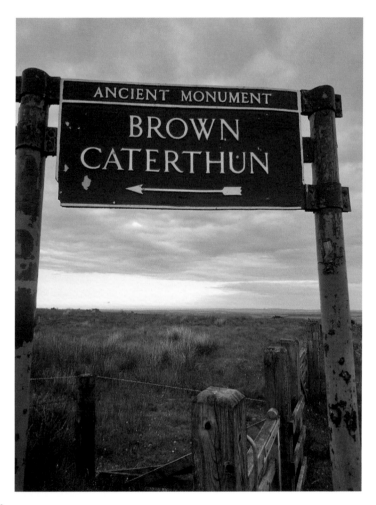

TURN BY TURN DIRECTIONS

Start from the small parking area at the White Caterthun.

1. Walk through gate and follow path toward the White Caterthun.
2. At 0.37 miles you reach the top.
3. Go back the same way you came.
4. At 0.75 miles cross the road and head up towards the Brown Caterthun.
5. At 1.31 miles you reach the top.
6. Walk back down again.
7. At 1.90 miles you return to the carpark area.

GLENCADAM DISTILLERY

Glencadam doesn't have a visitor centre yet, but they have big plans to create one. Until then they very much welcome anyone interested in distilleries and whisky; just email or phone them ahead and they will be happy to show you around. For now, they are giving pre-booked tours on Tuesdays and Thursdays. Be aware that kids are not allowed inside the distillery. There is a cosy sitting room with a TV that children are welcome to use while waiting for their parents.

Glencadam first opened in 1825 but was closed down during both world wars where the warehouses used to store whisky casks instead were used as barracks for soldiers. It finally opened again as a distillery in 2003 and single malt whisky was once again in production.

DRIVING DIRECTIONS

Glencadam Distillery can be a bit tricky to find. It is in the town of Brechin, but it's situated next to the Parkview Bowling Club on Smithbank Road.

PRACTICAL INFORMATION

DISTILLERY / WHISKY BAR
GLENCADAM DISTILLERY
Brechin
Angus, DD9 7PA
+44 (0) 1356 622217
sales@angusdundee.co.uk
www.glencadamwhisky.com

RESTAURANT / CAFÉ
Bring a picnic.

MORE INFORMATION ABOUT THE AREA
https://www.visitscotland.com/info/
towns-villages/brechin-p241581

ACCOMMODATION OPTION
GRAMARCY HOUSE
6 Airlie Street,
Brechin
Angus, DD9 6JP
+44 (0) 1356 622240

BEN VRACKIE

THE PERFECT MOUNTAIN FOR A FAMILY OUTING.

▷ **START AND END POINT**

CAR PARK AT BEN VRACKIE

✕ **DESTINATION**

BEN VRACKIE

◇ **WHISKY**

EDRADOUR
10 YO

▦ **DIFFICULTY**

MOUNTAIN HIKING

☆ **HIGHLIGHTS**

VIEW POINT AT THE BASE OF THE MOUNTAIN, THE TOP OF BEN VRACKIE

◷ **DURATION OF THE HIKE**

3.5 HOURS
5.7 MILES (9.1KM)

△ **ELEVATION GAIN**

2132 FEET
(650M)

SINGLE MALT

- GOLD
- DRIED FRUIT, ALMONDS
- SPICY CHRISTMAS CAKE, HONEY, ALMONDS
- OLOROSO SHERRY AND BOURBON

ALCOHOL **40** % CONTENT

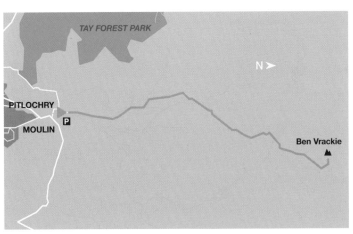

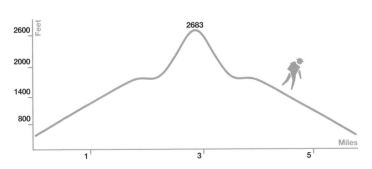

DESCRIPTION OF THE WALK

I am tempted to say that this is a great beginner's mountain, but it depends on the weather. If you do this walk during summertime, it's pretty easy: a mountain walk for all ages. If you plan on doing this walk during winter when there is snow, make sure to take precautions and bring the right gear for it, such as an ice axe, etc.

On the way up we made way for a very determined German in sandals – open sandals! We still talk about this sandal-wearing man long after this trip, wondering if he made it down again in one piece... I did this walk with my youngest son, he is 11 years old but has the stamina of an antelope (don't know where he gets it from, it's certainly not from me), and it was perfect for him.

Make sure to pack snacks and plenty of water. And, as usual, bring equipment for all kinds of weather.

Head off from the parking lot and walk up through the woodland until you reach a gate that leads into an open area towards the hills. Follow the trail up and around the hills. On your way you pass a bench. There you can look down on Pitlochry and Moulin. Then, walk on and at 3.5 km you reach the foot of Ben Vrackie and see the beautiful Loch a'Choire on your left. Head up the mountain when you are ready. The path is not too difficult and there is no doubt as to which way to walk up the mountain, but there are a lot of loose stones and rocks that you need to be aware of. Especially on your way down again the loose rubble can cause you to slip if you are not careful. Once on the top, you can have a well-earned rest by the rocks and look out on the world below. The view is simply stunning!

TIP

Do not wear open sandals up the mountains! Unless of course you are an ancient, immortal Greek god who has years and years of experience and is rocking the open sandal look.

TURN BY TURN DIRECTIONS

Start at the Ben Vrackie car park.

1. At 0.27 miles cross the gravel road and head through the gate. Walk on.
2. At 0.71 miles walk through the gate and head up towards the hill.
3. At 1.29 miles turn to the right.
4. At 1.74 miles walk straight ahead.
5. At 2.04 miles walk straight ahead.
6. At 2.11 miles you reach Loch a'Choire.
7. At 2.18 miles start walking upwards.
8. At 2.84 miles you reach the top.
9. Head down the same way.
10. At 5.67 miles you are back at the parking area.

EDRADOUR DISTILLERY

As one of the smaller distilleries in Scotland, Edradour is definitely one to visit. It's charming and the whisky is amazing (and the tour guides have a great sense of humour; that's always a bonus).

With this distillery you don't have to book in advance, unless you are a large group. Just ask for a guided tour when you arrive. They are open Monday to Saturday, but check online before you visit, just to be sure. The only thing you need to be aware of is the age limit. Where many other distilleries accept small children, this distillery does not. You will need to be above 18 years of age, and you should bring ID just in case you need to prove it. If in doubt, check their website or send them an email; they are all very friendly and will be happy to be of assistance.

DRIVING DIRECTIONS

Edradour Distillery is situated a few miles from Pitlochry centre. Follow the A924 Braemar/Blairgowrie through Moulin and you see signs towards the distillery. If you have GPS use the postcode PH16 5JP.

To get to Ben Vrackie from the distillery you just need to follow the A924 to Moulin, and you can find the parking area at the end of Baledmund Road.

PRACTICAL INFORMATION

DISTILLERY / WHISKY BAR
EDRADOUR DISTILLERY
Pitlochry
Perth and Kinross, PH16 5JP
+44 (0) 1796 472095
tours@edradour.com
info@edradour.com
www.edradour.com

RESTAURANT / CAFÉ
Bring a picnic.

MORE INFORMATION ABOUT THE AREA
https://www.pitlochry.org

ACCOMMODATION OPTION
There are a lot of accommodation options in the area; www.pitlochry.org has a great list.

ABERLOUR

A LOVELY WATERFALL WALK.

▷ START AND END POINT	✕ DESTINATION
THE GLENALLACHIE DISTILLERY	**THE MASH TUN**

✎ WHISKY	▦ DIFFICULTY
THE GLENALLACHIE CASK STRENGTH 10 YO	**WALKING**

☆ HIGHLIGHTS	◷ DURATION OF THE HIKE
THE WATERFALL, CREEPY CEMETERY	**1.5 HOURS 3.5 MILES** (5.5KM)
	⌂ ELEVATION GAIN
	505 FEET (154M)

ALCOHOL **54.8%** CONTENT

CASK STRENGTH SINGLE MALT

👁	CARAMEL
👃	VANILLA, RAISINS, HONEY, ORANGE
👅	SPICES, ORANGE, TREACLE, RAISINS
🛢	CHARRED AMERICAN OAK; ENRICHED IN PEDRO XIMENEZ BARRELS

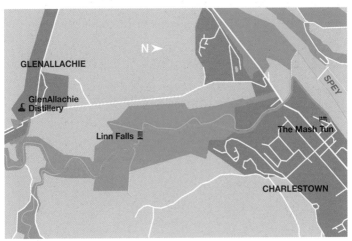

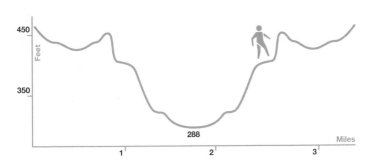

DESCRIPTION OF THE WALK

A lovely walk from and to GlenAllachie Distillery that can be expanded into a much longer walk if you wish: This walk can be combined with the "Mash Tun and the Woodland Walk" (see next chapter).

Park at the distillery, make sure to let them know you are there, and head off towards Aberlour via an idyllic waterfall route. Follow the turn-by-turn directions and you soon find yourself by a lovely waterfall in the woods; a perfect spot for a picnic if you fancy it, otherwise continue onwards towards the whisky bar Mash Tun. When you get to the main road you see the cemetery on the other side. Follow the path around it and forward under the bridge and soon you reach the Mash Tun.

If you are hungry, the Mash Tun serves really good food, so it is a good place to stop for lunch, but I really recommend picnicking if the weather is nice and warm. The setting is like something taken right out of a fairy tale.

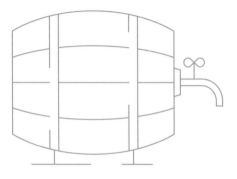

Here is a fun fact for all soda lovers out there (and anyone that likes fun facts). Aberlour is the birthplace of Scottish-born entrepreneur and pharmacist Alexander Cameron Sim (1840–1900) who moved overseas to work at the Naval Hospital in Hong Kong. After a few years, he moved on to Nagasaki, and then Kobe, where he – hold on – invented "Ramune": the Japanese soda with the marble at the top of the bottle neck that needs to be pushed down in order to open the bottle. Ramune is loved by many children and adults today all over the world. On a side note, he also built a fire lookout tower, organised a volunteer firefighting group, and helped with organising relief and support efforts following two of the most devastating earthquakes in Japanese history.

TURN BY TURN DIRECTIONS

Start from the parking area at the distillery.

1. From the distillery head towards the road and go left, and after 0.02 miles go right.
2. At 0.20 miles you see a sign on the left saying "Footpath to Aberlour". Climb the small wooden steps
3. over the fence and follow the path with the river on your left side.
4. At 0.84 miles you reach the waterfall. At the bottom, go right and follow the river as before.
5. At 1.42 miles you reach a road. Cross it and walk around the cemetery. Continue forward under the bridge.
6. At 1.73 miles you reach The Mash Tun.
7. At this point you can choose to stop for lunch here and walk back the same way you came.
   Or you can combine this walk with the next whisky walk and head on.
8. At 5.56 km / 3.46 miles you have returned to the distillery.

GLENALLACHIE DISTILLERY

This is a lovely little distillery with a drive and a passion that flows into their whisky. Even though the competition in the whisky world is fierce, this distillery chooses to slow down and do everything carefully, from the fermentation time to maturation. Choose between their "Wee Allachie" tour that gives you a one-hour guided tour, or the "Connoisseurs" tour that takes two hours and gives you a journey behind the scenes including a visit to the warehouse. Open Monday to Friday, but check their website in advance to avoid disappointment.

DRIVING DIRECTIONS

Take the A95 towards Aberlour, take a left towards GlenAllachie,
and you will see signs towards the distillery.

PRACTICAL INFORMATION

DISTILLERY / WHISKY BAR
THE GLENALLACHIE DISTILLERY
Aberlour
Banffshire, AB38 9LR
+44 (0) 1340 872547
info@glenallachie.com
www.theglenallachie.com

RESTAURANT / CAFÉ
THE MASH TUN
8 Broomfield Square,
Aberlour
Banffshire, AB38 9QP
+44 (0) 1340 881771
info@mashtun-aberlour.com
www.mashtun-aberlour.com

MORE INFORMATION ABOUT THE AREA
www.speysidevisitorcentre.scot

ACCOMMODATION OPTION
THE MASH TUN
(see above)

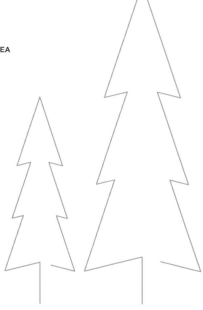

MASH TUN

A GLORIOUS WOODLAND WALK.

▷ START AND END POINT	✕ DESTINATION
THE MASH TUN	**THE WOODS**

🏷 WHISKY	▦ DIFFICULTY
GLENFARCLAS 15 YO	**WALKING**

☆ HIGHLIGHTS	⊙ DURATION OF THE HIKE
WALK THROUGH THE WOODS	**2.5 HOURS** **5.2 MILES** (8.3KM)
	△ ELEVATION GAIN
	843 FEET (257M)

HIGHLAND SINGLE MALT SCOTCH WHISKY

ALCOHOL **46 %** CONTENT

GOLDEN AMBER

BUTTERSCOTCH FRUIT

MALT, FRUITCAKE, SHERRY, ORANGE PEEL

SHERRY CASK

Glenfarclas

HIGHLAND SINGLE MALT SCOTCH WHISKY

AGED 15 YEARS

700ML ℮

46% VOL

LOREM IPSUM DOLOR SIT AMET IPSUM DOLOR SIT AMET, CONSECTETUER ADIPISCING ELIT, SED

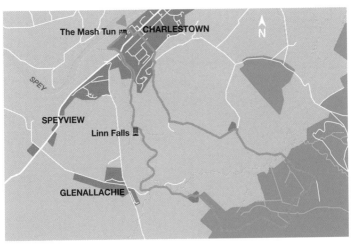

The Mash Tun · CHARLESTOWN

SPEY

SPEYVIEW

Linn Falls

GLENALLACHIE

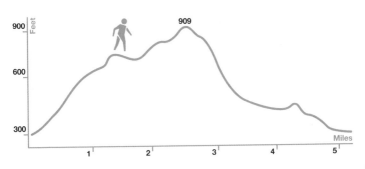

909

900 Feet

600

300

Miles

1 2 3 4 5

DESCRIPTION OF THE WALK

Regardless of whether you have already done the walk from the last chapter or you start with this one, your starting point will be the Mash Tun. There is parking at this whisky bar, but check carefully if there is a fee. Eat a hearty meal and enjoy a whisky and set off towards the woods.

Follow the turn-by-turn directions and you get to a woodland area that oozes peace and tranquillity. At one point you have the choice to walk straight ahead towards the GlenAllachie distillery or back towards Aberlour and the Mash Tun. If you choose to combine this walk with the "GlenAl-lachie and the Walk to Aberlour" you need to continue straight ahead when you reach the river and the wooden steps again. If you are doing this walk only, continue following the turn-by-turn directions and you get back to the Mash Tun.

TURN BY TURN DIRECTIONS

Start at the Mash Tun.

1. Go right; walk up to the main road.
2. At 0.06 miles go left.
3. At 0.09 miles turn right and follow the road.
4. At 0.34 miles turn left.
5. At 0.35 miles go right and uphill and follow the path.
6. At 0.80 miles go left and follow the path.
7. At 1.32 miles go right and follow the path into the forest.
8. At 2.04 miles turn right.
9. At 2.84 miles go right.
10. At 3.25 miles go left.
11. At 3.35 miles go right.
12. At 3.54 miles go left.
13. At 3.65 miles walk right and over the wooden steps.
14. The river is on your left side. (This is the place where you can continue straight ahead if you want to return to the distillery. It is very close by.)
15. At 4.30 miles you reach the waterfall. At the bottom, walk right and follow the river as before.
16. At 4.87 miles you reach a road. Cross it and walk around the cemetery. Continue forward under the bridge.
17. At 5.18 miles you reach the Mash Tun.

THE MASH TUN

On the banks of the River Spey in Aberlour you can find the whisky bar The Mash Tun. Its owner has a great passion for whisky. This passion you can see the very minute you step inside: Most of the walls are either covered with shelves full of whisky or with decorations to do with whisky. Their menu offers suggestions as to which whisky to pair with the food. A bespoke tutored tasting is available if you like, just write or call ahead to set it up.

While you are there you should give yourself some time to admire the impressive Glenfarclas family cask collection which contains 51 single cask whiskies. There is no doubt that this is a serious whisky bar.

The Mash Tun is popular and it can be crowded, so if you prefer to visit while it's quiet give them a call and make a reservation. They also rent out rooms, so if you are feeling tired after your whisky tasting you can make sure there will not be a long walk to bed.

DRIVING DIRECTIONS

Finding the Mash Tun is easy. Aberlour is just north of Dufftown and the A95 runs straight through it. When on the high street in Aberlour, go down Elchies Road and you reach the Mash Tun at the end of the road. It is close to the Speyside Way Visitor Centre.

PRACTICAL INFORMATION

DISTILLERY / WHISKY BAR
THE MASH TUN
8 Broomfield Square
Aberlour
Banffshire, AB38 9QP
+44 (0) 1340 881771
info@mashtun-aberlour.com
www.mashtun-aberlour.com

RESTAURANT / CAFÉ
THE MASH TUN
(see information above)

MORE INFORMATION ABOUT THE AREA
www.speysidevisitorcentre.scot

ACCOMMODATION OPTION
THE MASH TUN
(see information above)

SWAN LAKE

A SHORT AND IDYLLIC WALK.

▷ START AND END POINT

THE LAKE AT BRODIE CASTLE

✕ DESTINATION

BRODIE CASTLE

🏷 WHISKY

BENROMACH
15 YO

▦ DIFFICULTY

WALKING

☆ HIGHLIGHTS

THE LAKE, THE CASTLE

🕐 DURATION OF THE HIKE

0.75 HOUR
1.7 MILES (2.8KM)

⼈ ELEVATION GAIN

85 FEET
(26M)

ALCOHOL
43 %
CONTENT

SPEYSIDE
SINGLE MALT

GOLDEN AMBER	
VANILLA, ORANGE, GINGER, SHERRY, PEAT	
FRUIT CAKE, APPLES, NUTMEG, PEAT	
SHERRY AND BOURBON	

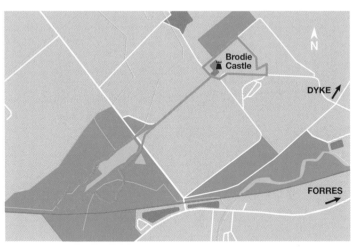

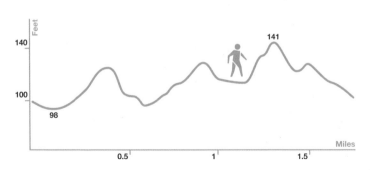

DESCRIPTION OF THE WALK

There are many picturesque castles in Scotland, and you can combine a visit to most of them with a nice walk, just like this one. Brodie Castle is old, gorgeous, and has turrets (we all like a few turrets on our castles, don't we?). You can walk the gardens free of charge, and if you like and it's open you can tour the castle as well for a fee. They have an art collection of old Dutch masters as well as more modern pieces.

The walk itself starts around the lovely lake where you can see swans if you're lucky, and it continues around the castle grounds. Follow the turn-by-turn directions and you can't go wrong.

Should you have some extra time on your hand, and if you have children with you (or if your inner child is bursting to come out) you can visit the Playful Garden, a garden especially for children. It is loads of fun for kids as well as adults.

The castle's café has a great selection of sandwiches and cakes, and their coffee is tasty.

If you fancy staying put in this idyllic environment, you can book a lodge on the castle grounds which is available to rent.

=========== **DID YOU KNOW?** ===========

It is said that there are three main ingredients in single malt whisky: barley, water, and yeast. But there is a fourth element that is absolutely essential to the makings of a great whisky – the cask!

TURN BY TURN DIRECTIONS

1. Take the path south-west and follow it around the lake.
2. At 0.68 miles go through the gate. Cross the road and go through another gate towards the castle.
3. At 0.96 miles walk left around the castle.
4. At 1.02 miles you reach the café.
5. At 1.12 miles take the path to the right.
6. At 1.26 miles go right towards the parking lot. When you reach the road walk right towards the castle.
7. At 1.44 miles walk down towards the lake again.
8. At 1.72 miles walk through the gate and cross the road.
9. At 1.73 miles you are back where you started.

BENROMACH DISTILLERY

Benromach is a distillery with its feet planted firmly on the ground and with a passion for making whisky by hand. They proudly avoid computers and other gadgets in order to make the best whisky possible the old-fashioned way. They have several tours for you to choose from, just go online and pick the tour you would like and send a request or give them a call.

DRIVING DIRECTIONS

Drive off A96 to take C9E at Brodie and park by the lake.

PRACTICAL INFORMATION

DISTILLERY / WHISKY BAR
BENROMACH DISTILLERY COMPANY LTD.
Invererne Road
Forres
Moray, IV36 3EB
+44 (0) 1309 675968
info@benromach.com
www.benromach.com

RESTAURANT / CAFÉ
BRODIE CASTLE
Forres
Moray, IV36 2TE
+44 (0) 1309 641371
brodiecastle@nts.org.uk
www.nts.org.uk/visit/places/brodie-castle

MORE INFORMATION ABOUT THE AREA
www.nts.org.uk/visit/places/brodie-castle

ACCOMMODATION OPTION
CORMACK LODGE
Brodie Castle
Forres
Moray, IV36 2TE
+44 (0) 1314 580305
https://www.nts.org.uk/Holidays/Accommoda-
tion/Cormack-Lodge-Brodie-Castle

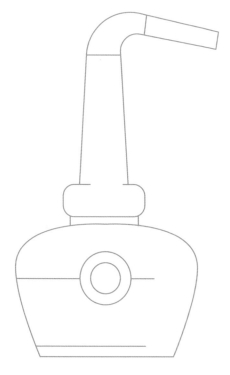

VALLEY RIVER

A MARVELLOUS WHISKY VALLEY WALK.

▷ START AND END POINT

BALLINDALLOCH DISTILLERY

✕ DESTINATION

THE RIVER AVON

🏷 WHISKY

CRAGGANMORE 1986

▦ DIFFICULTY

WALKING

☆ HIGHLIGHTS

THE RIVER PICNIC SPOT

☉ DURATION OF THE HIKE

1 HOUR
2.2 MILES (3.5KM)

△ ELEVATION GAIN

101 FEET
(31M)

SINGLE MALT

ALCOHOL **53.1%** CONTENT

Ballindalloch
Cragganmore 1986
700ml 53.1%
13/09121

👁	AMBER
👃	SPICE, CHOCOLATE
👅	SPICE, CHOCOLATE, HONEY
🛢	BOURBON CASK

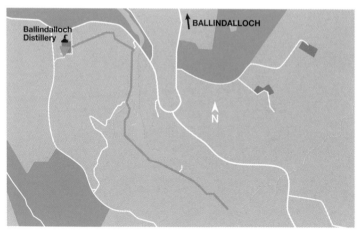

Ballindalloch Distillery

BALLINDALLOCH

N

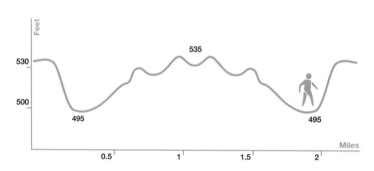

Feet

530

500

535

495

495

0.5   1   1.5   2

Miles

DESCRIPTION OF THE WALK

There is something both lively and peaceful about this river walk. Although you will pass by a golf course, the likelihood of you meeting anyone beyond that point is small, and this gives the river the chance to enchant you with its natural scintillating flow. At one point the river is divided by a tiny island in the middle, and this is where you (on your side of the river) can find a bench hidden in the bushes: a perfect place to have a picnic.

Let the distillery know if you are parking in their parking area and then follow the turn-by-turn directions and enjoy the tranquillity of the area. When you are ready to return, head back the same way you came and walk towards the distillery.

As there is no café at the distillery and there are no pubs along the walk, bringing a picnic is a great idea. If you have time and the weather is not ideal to eat outside, you can visit Ballindalloch Castle and have lunch in their tea room and afterwards tour the castle and gardens.

At Ballindalloch Distillery there are only four employees and three of them work in production!

TURN BY TURN DIRECTIONS

Start at the path at the north-east corner of the distillery. It is just on the edge of the golf course.

1. Walk for 0.17 miles until you reach a driveway. Go right.
2. At 0.27 miles go right and follow the path.
3. At 1.09 miles walk down a tiny path to the river. This is the perfect picnic spot.
4. Return the same way you came.
5. At 2.19 miles you return to the distillery.

BALLINDALLOCH DISTILLERY

With all the fierce competition in the whisky business, you have to offer the customers something special to stand out, and the Ballindalloch Distillery certainly does that. Their tours are adjusted to the visitors so that whisky connoisseurs don't get bored by hearing facts they already know, and whisky beginners get a tour that explains everything one would like to know about whisky production.

This in itself is a great idea, but that's not all – Ballindalloch also offers cake! Any tour that starts with coffee and cake definitely has me enthralled. Joking aside, the coffee-and-cake introduction gives a homey feeling, and it is a great way to start a tour.

As the distillery is new, the whisky was not yet ready when I visited, but soon we can all taste the fruits of their hard work. But do not fear; even if you visit earlier than the whisky is ready, they still offer whisky tasting. Tastings of the Macpherson-Grant family's own private casks are offered. Which casks you get to taste will change with time, but they are all delicious. If you are driving or don't want to drink, there is no charge for your tour, but – between you and I – bring some of those empty driver's bottles because you don't want to miss out on this tasting!

DRIVING DIRECTIONS

The distillery is just off the A95 at Ballindalloch and the Bridge of Avon.

PRACTICAL INFORMATION

DISTILLERY / WHISKY BAR
BALLINDALLOCH DISTILLERY
Ballindalloch
Banffshire, AB37 9AA
+44 (0) 1807 500331
enquiries@ballindallochdistillery.com
www.ballindallochdistillery.com

RESTAURANT / CAFÉ
Bring a picnic or
eat at the Ballindalloch Castle tea room.
www.ballindallochcastle.co.uk

MORE INFORMATION ABOUT THE AREA
http://www.glenlivet-cairngorms.co.uk

ACCOMMODATION OPTION
THE DELNASHAUGH HOTEL
Ballindalloch
Banffshire, AB37 9AS
+44 (0) 1807 500379
enquiries@delnashaughhotel.com
https://www.delnashaughhotel.com

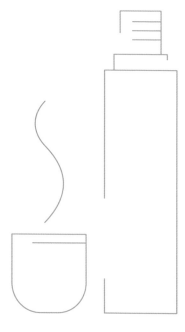

BEN RINNES

A WEE HILL WALK FOLLOWED BY AMAZING WHISKY.

▷ START AND END POINT

PARK BY ROAD

✕ DESTINATION

BEN RINNES

🏷 WHISKY

GLENFARCLAS
25 YO

🗺 DIFFICULTY

MOUNTAIN HIKING

☆ HIGHLIGHTS

THE MOUNTAIN TOP

🕐 DURATION OF THE HIKE

2.5 HOURS
4.7 MILES (7.5KM)

⋀ ELEVATION GAIN

1650 FEET
(503M)

ALCOHOL
43 %
CONTENT

SINGLE MALT

AMBER

MARMALADE,
HONEY, SHERRY,
OAK

OAK, SHERRY,
MALT, CHOCOLATE

OLOROSO SHERRY

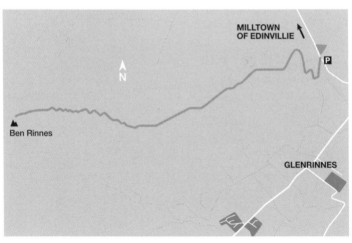

MILLTOWN
OF EDINVILLIE

P

N

Ben Rinnes

GLENRINNES

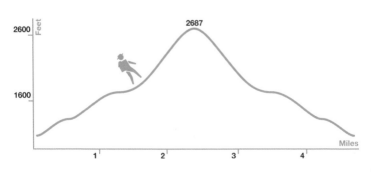

Feet

2600

2687

1600

Miles

1   2   3   4

DESCRIPTION OF THE WALK

Now, before I did this walk, I heard a rumour that this trail is great for running. I did not believe it until I saw it with my own eyes. The Scottish people truly are a fierce bunch! I saw a man running up the mountain faster than his dog. The man did not have time to stop, he called out to me, he was training. And then he whistled at his dog, telling it to hurry up. Need I say more?

Well, for all of us who are not so fierce, and especially for people who are not used to mountains (for example, everyone out of shape and visiting from a flat land… like me) it is perfectly okay to walk all the way up.

The parking area can be a bit tricky to spot, it's basically just a tiny bit of space at the side of the road, but the gate with the info board is there so you will know that it's the right place. Even though the distillery lies just at the bottom of Ben Rinnes, you must drive around the mountain in order to get to the path. It is worth it.

Enter through the gate and head up. The path up is not so difficult, but there is a lot of loose rubble so be careful. This hike is best done in good weather, but it is also doable in rain and snow, just take the necessary precautions. You will be walking up a smaller hill first and then down a bit only to go up again. Just follow the path and you will not get lost. The view from the top is, as expected, spectacular, especially on a clear day. Enjoy!

DID YOU KNOW?

The Scottish people are wonderful and robust. They are used to harsh weather conditions and difficult walks. What might seem like a mountain to people from other countries will probably be a wee hill to them.

TURN BY TURN DIRECTIONS

1. Park and head through the gate and up the hill.
2. At 1.18 miles you have reached the top of Roys Hill.
3. Follow the path for 2.34 miles until you reach the top of Ben Rinnes.
4. Walk back the same way.
5. At 4.70 miles you arrive back at the beginning.

GLENFARCLAS DISTILLERY

Nestled at the foot of Ben Rinnes lies the distillery Glenfarclas. It has been in the same family since 1865. Through six generations, the Grant family has been committed to making Highland single malt in the traditional Speyside style. You can feel the age and provenance in the whisky as well as in the distillery. They opened their visitor centre in 1973 and you can tell that they know how to give a good whisky tour, full of fun and history. Choose between the "Classic Tour", the "Connoisseur's Tour", and the "Five Decades Tour". Send an email to book. The staff is also very helpful so if you have any questions just contact them.

DRIVING DIRECTIONS

From Glenfarclas Distillery, take the A95 north-east and at Aberlour veterinary centre take a right and then follow the road until you spot the gate that leads up the path.

PRACTICAL INFORMATION

DISTILLERY / WHISKY BAR
GLENFARCLAS DISTILLERY
Ballindalloch
Banffshire, AB37 9BD
+44 (0) 1807 500345
info@glenfarclas.com
www.glenfarclas.com

RESTAURANT / CAFÉ
Bring a picnic.

MORE INFORMATION ABOUT THE AREA
http://www.glenlivet-cairngorms.co.uk

ACCOMMODATION OPTION
THE DELNASHAUGH HOTEL
Ballindalloch
Banffshire, AB37 9AS
+44 (0) 1807 500379
enquiries@delnashaughhotel.com
https://www.delnashaughhotel.com

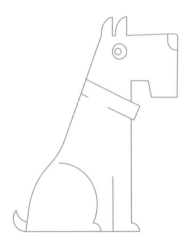

INSH MARSHES

A PICTURESQUE DISTILLERY AND AN EQUALLY PICTURESQUE WALK.

▷ START AND END POINT

SPEYSIDE DISTILLERY

✕ DESTINATION

INSH MARSHES

🏷 WHISKY

SPEY TENNÉ

🀫 DIFFICULTY

WALKING

☆ HIGHLIGHTS

PASTURES WITH ANIMALS, BIRD HIDES, VIEWPOINT & PICNIC AREA

⏲ DURATION OF THE HIKE

1.5 HOURS
3.5 MILES (5.7KM)

⌂ ELEVATION GAIN

375 FEET
(112M)

ALCOHOL
46 %
CONTENT

SINGLE MALT

👁 **COPPER ROSÉ**

👃 **FRUIT, FLOWERS**

👄 **PEACH, ALMONDS**

🛢 **BOURBON AND TAWNY PORT CASKS**

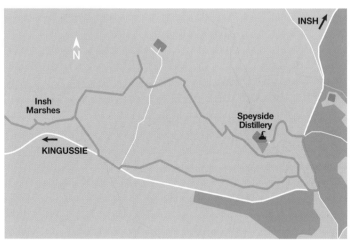

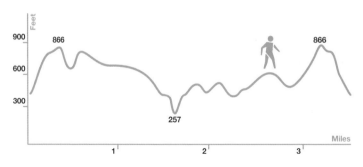

DESCRIPTION OF THE WALK

Park at the distillery and let them know that you are setting off on your walk. Head back up to the main road and to the right. Follow the turn-by-turn directions and soon you are walking in lush pastures. If you are an animal lover you will be pleased to know that you may meet cows as well as horses on your walk. The cows are in pastures that you walk through, the horses' pasture you can't enter, but you can talk to them over the fence. Both the horses and the cows are very friendly but please be aware to never go near calves and to leash your dog if you have one with you to make sure there is no danger.

After a bit more than two kilometres, you reach the path to the bird hide (why not bring your binoculars?). After that, head on to the next bird hide, and a little later you reach a great spot for a picnic. There are also plenty of other opportunities to enjoy a packed lunch along the way, if the weather permits it.

Head back to the path and go back to the distillery as described in the turn-by-turn directions.

TURN BY TURN DIRECTIONS

1. Walk back to the main road from the distillery.
2. At 0.19 miles turn right.
3. At 0.40 miles go right and walk through the gate.
4. At 0.45 miles walk left along the path.
5. At 0.53 miles follow the path straight ahead.
6. At 1.08 miles cross the path and enter the gate onto the pasture.
7. Cross the pasture.
8. At 1.32 miles walk through the gate, go left, and follow the path.
9. At 1.32 miles go right and walk to the bird hide.
10. At 1.47 miles you reach the bird hide. Walk back along the same path.
11. At 1.48 miles go right.
12. At 1.52 miles turn right at the next path and follow it towards the next bird hide.
13. At 1.62 miles you reach the second bird hide.
14. Go back the same way; at.72 miles turn left and continue along the path.
15. At 1.77 miles take a left and follow the path.
16. At 1.88 miles walk straight ahead.
17. At 2.18 miles go left.
18. At 2.26 miles you reach a viewpoint that's a good picnic spot.
19. Go back to the path.
20. At 2.32 miles go left.
21. At 2.72 miles go left.
22. At 2.76 miles turn right and follow the path.
23. At 3.09 miles go left.
24. At 3.14 miles you reach a road. Go through the gate and walk left.
25. At 3.35 miles go left towards the distillery.
26. At 3.54 miles you reach the distillery again.

SPEYSIDE DISTILLERY

Tucked in between the magnificent Cairngorm Mountains lies the pretty little distillery of Speyside. Once a barley mill, it is now a single malt distillery where a passionate team of experts crafts high-quality whisky.

They offer visits by appointment only, as it is a small distillery, so if you would like visit then send them an email or give them a call. You should also check their event calendar as they regularly host exciting events. When planning your visit, make sure to check the "How to Find Us" section on their website first.

They have a lot of different whiskies for you to taste and my advice is: Be adventurous when you choose which whisky to try – you might be in for a pleasant surprise.

DRIVING DIRECTIONS

This distillery is on the B970 off the A86 in Kingussie.

PRACTICAL INFORMATION

DISTILLERY / WHISKY BAR
SPEYSIDE DISTILLERY
Duchess Road
Kingussie, 3XFW+4X
+44 (0) 1479 810126
info@speysidedistillers.co.uk
www.speysidedistillery.co.uk

RESTAURANT / CAFÉ
Bring a picnic.

MORE INFORMATION ABOUT THE AREA
www.visitcairngorms.com/kingussie

ACCOMMODATION OPTION
OSPREY LODGE
2 Invertromie Steading
Kingussie, PH21 1NS
+44 (0) 7807 001084
contact@ospreylodgescotland.co.uk
www.ospreylodgescotland.co.uk

POLEWOOD

AN ENCHANTED FOREST WALK.

▷ START AND END POINT	✕ DESTINATION
DUFFTOWN PARKING AREA	**POLEWOOD**

◇ WHISKY	▦ DIFFICULTY
SPEYSIDE COOPERAGE 10 YO	**WALKING**

☆ HIGHLIGHTS	◔ DURATION OF THE HIKE
THE GIANT'S CHAIR, THE FAIRY VILLAGE, FOREST WALK	**1.5 HOURS** **3.3 MILES** (5.3KM)
	⋀ ELEVATION GAIN
	338 FEET (103M)

SINGLE MALT

40 % ALCOHOL CONTENT

👁 LIGHT GOLD

👃 FRUIT, HONEY

👅 FRUIT, PEPPER-CORN, BARLEY SUGAR

🛢 A SECRET

SPEYSIDE COOPERAGE

Acorn to Cask

10 YEAR OLD
SPEYSIDE SINGLE MALT
SCOTCH WHISKY

PRODUCT OF SCOTLAND
SPEYSIDE COOPERAGE
CRAIGELLACHIE, AB38 9RS

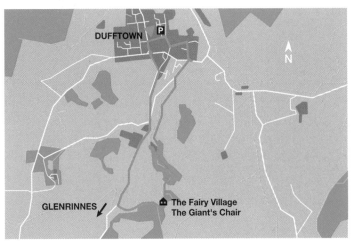

DUFFTOWN

GLENRINNES

The Fairy Village
The Giant's Chair

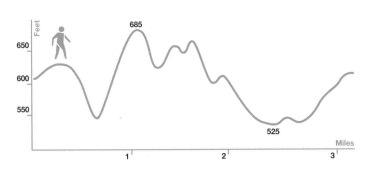

DESCRIPTION OF THE WALK

Do you believe in fairies? After going on this walk, you just might. I'm happy I brought all my kids with me on this trip as it turned out to be so much more fun than we had anticipated. We went in search of the Giant's Chair, a rock shaped with time by the water of River Dullan, but ended up finding funny stones, a meditating elephant, dinosaurs, and a fairy village. Although the Giant's Chair was fascinating, it was the elephants, the engraved stones, and the fairy village that made this walk extra special for us.

Follow the turn-by-turn directions that will lead you to the forest. Once in the forest, keep your eyes open and explore to your heart's content and when you're done, get back on track with the turn-by-turn directions and head on back to the starting point.

It is more fun if the sun is out, but the experience is enchanting in all kinds of weather.

You could bring lunch with you as you will walk past a bench close to the forest that is perfect for a lunch break, but they also have a café at the Cooperage. Choices, choices... Enjoy!

The world record for building a 190-litre barrel is 3 minutes 3 seconds! The world record holder is working at the Cooperage and if you are lucky you can watch him in action.

TURN BY TURN DIRECTIONS

Start at the parking area.

1. Walk left at Albert Place and left again at Balvenie Street.
2. Walk past the clock tower and further along Church Street.
3. At 1.28 miles turn left along the path. Continue along this path.
4. At 2.45 miles walk straight ahead along the path.
5. At 2.71 miles you reach a bigger road. Continue along the road.
6. At 2.83 miles you reach an even bigger road; turn left here.
7. At 2.87 miles go right onto a path and follow it leftward.
8. At 2.93 miles you reach a road. Turn right.
9. At 2.98 miles go left.
10. At 3.11 miles walk straight ahead.
11. At 3.19 miles go left.
12. At 3.26 miles you are back where you started.

SPEYSIDE COOPERAGE

One of the most important factors in making a great whisky is the cask. At Speyside Cooperage they produce and repair around 150 000 casks a year and when the cask is no longer usable, what is left gets used for items that sell in the gift shop, and thus makes the life cycle of a cask even longer.

Choose between two tours: a classic tour, and a VIP tour. On the VIP tour you get a closer look at the coopers at work, being on the ground where the magic happens, but you will need to be above 18 years old for this tour. To book a tour, send an email or call. Once you've taken it all in you can enjoy a bite of lunch in their café and browse around in their gift shop.

DRIVING DIRECTIONS

To get from the Cooperage to the beginning of the walk, drive right on A941 and drive to Dufftown centre where you park at the parking area at Albert Place.

PRACTICAL INFORMATION

DISTILLERY / WHISKY BAR
SPEYSIDE COOPERAGE
Dufftown Road
Craigellachie
Banffshire, AB38 9RS
+44 (0) 1340 871108
enquiries@speysidecooperage.co.uk
www.speysidecooperage.co.uk

RESTAURANT / CAFÉ
THE SPEYSIDE COOPERAGE
(see information above)

MORE INFORMATION ABOUT THE AREA
www.greaterspeyside.com

ACCOMMODATION OPTION
THE HIGHLANDER INN
Craigellachie
Banffshire, AB38 9SR
+44 (0) 1340 881446
info@whiskyinn.com
www.whiskyinn.com

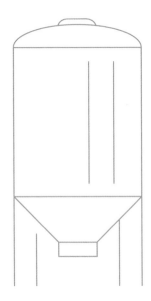

CNOC CASTLE

WHISKY, ROCKS, SHEEP, AND… MORE ROCKS.

▷ **START AND END POINT**

TORABHAIG DISTILLERY

✕ **DESTINATION**

CNOC CASTLE

🏷 **WHISKY**

MOSSBURN BLENDED WHISKY

▦ **DIFFICULTY**

WALKING

☆ **HIGHLIGHTS**

THE RUINS OF CNOC CASTLE, THE VIEW FROM CNOC CASTLE, THE COAST

⊙ **DURATION OF THE HIKE**

1 HOUR
1.4 MILES (2.3KM)

⌃ **ELEVATION GAIN**

220 FEET
(67M)

BLENDED MALT

ALCOHOL 40 % CONTENT

👁 LIGHT GOLD

👃 FRUIT, HONEY

👅 FRUIT, PEPPER-CORN, BARLEY SUGAR

🛢 N/A

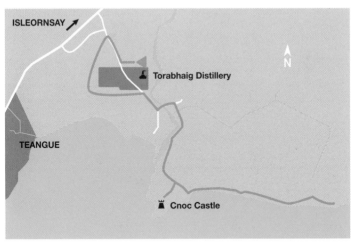

ISLEORNSAY

Torabhaig Distillery

TEANGUE

Cnoc Castle

N

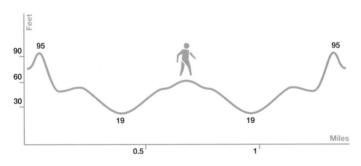

Feet

95

95

90

60

30

19

19

0.5

1

Miles

DESCRIPTION OF THE WALK

There is something special about those walks where you don't meet a single soul on your way. It is almost like you have entered another realm. This walk is bound to be one of those.

Park at the distillery parking lot and let the staff know you are there, then head up towards the road. Just before you reach the road, turn left and walk down the path that leads you around the distillery. You might think at first that this can't possibly lead to anywhere special but keep on walking. When you reach the bridge, you cross it and instead of going through the gate straight ahead you go right through the bushes and onward. It's a bendy path and if it's raining or has been raining not long ago you might have to jump over small streams and puddles. Eventually, you reach the opening, and a flock of sheep will look at you like they have never seen a human being before (they have).

On the top of the small hill are the remains of Cnoc Castle and on a clear day there is an amazing view. Walk up there but be careful.

Leave the sheep behind and head to the rocky beach. Be prepared for a difficult walk and be careful to look out for slippery stones and rocks; it looks gorgeous, but it does not take much to slip and sprain one's ankle. A pair of good walking boots will come in handy on this walk. Depending on the tide, it might be possible to keep walking along the coast; if not, just follow the turn-by-turn directions and go back to the distillery for a hearty lunch at their café.

TIP

Good hiking shoes or boots can make or break your trip, so make sure you are properly geared up. If in doubt ask your local outdoor gear shop.

TURN BY TURN DIRECTIONS

Start from the distillery parking lot.

1. Walk back towards the road.
2. At 0.06 miles, turn left down the small gravel road towards the sea and then follow the path up to the bridge.
3. At 0.27 miles cross the bridge to the left and at the steel fence head right down a tiny fern path.
4. Follow the tiny path across water and mud puddles.
5. At 0.34 miles you reach a clearing and can now see the ruins of Cnoc Castle.
6. Go up to the castle through the gap in the fence.
7. Follow the coastline until 0.73 miles.
8. Head back the same way.
9. At 1.41 miles you arrive back at the parking lot.

TORABHAIG DISTILLERY

As one of the new distilleries in Scotland, Torabhaig's very first whisky is new. They started distilling in 2017 and in 2020 their whisky was ready. The newly renovated buildings are a joy to look at, and in the building across from the visitor centre they have a café with a great lunch menu. And their coffee is good, I can assure you. You can book a guided tour online, but be aware that in this distillery the tour is only for people who are 13 years and older. If you have any questions about the distillery or even about walking in the area ask at reception; the team is very friendly and happy to help and knows the area very well.

DRIVING DIRECTIONS

You find the distillery just outside Teangue off the A851.

PRACTICAL INFORMATION

DISTILLERY / WHISKY BAR
TORABHAIG DISTILLERY LTD
Teangue
Sleat
Isle of Skye, IV44 8RE
+44 (0) 1471 833447
info@torabhaig.com
www.torabhaig.com

RESTAURANT / CAFÉ
TORABHAIG DISTILLERY
(see information above)

MORE INFORMATION ABOUT THE AREA
www.isleofskye.com

ACCOMMODATION OPTION
UIG HOTEL
Uig
Isle of Skye, IV51 9YE
+44 (0) 1470 542205
www.uig-hotel-skye.com

RAASAY

A GLORIOUS WALK ON AN ISLAND THAT LEAVES YOU WANTING TO STAY FOREVER.

▷ START AND END POINT

HALLAIG ROAD

✕ DESTINATION

HALLAIG

🏷 WHISKY

WHILE WE WAIT

🁢 DIFFICULTY

WALKING

☆ HIGHLIGHTS

THE VIEW OVER THE SEA, HALLAIG VILLAGE (ABANDONED)

☉ DURATION OF THE HIKE

2 HOURS 3.8 MILES (6KM)

⌅ ELEVATION GAIN

630 FEET (192M)

SINGLE MALT

👁	AMBER
👃	PEAT, BERRIES, MELON
👅	ORANGE ZEST, RED WINE, OAK
🛢	FRESH OAK AND TUSCAN WINE CASKS

ALCOHOL **46 %** CONTENT

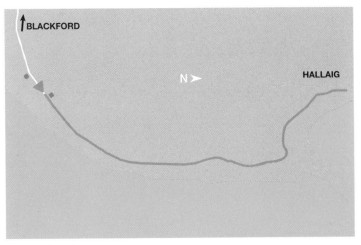

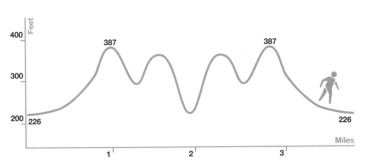

DESCRIPTION OF THE WALK

Raasay is an enchanting little island. We found the small town of Clachan very nice, but it was the second we started our walk among the high cliffs covered in huge ferns that the island really became outstanding for us. It felt as if we had been stranded on a deserted jungle island and I almost expected dinosaurs to appear through the branches of the big trees, trampling on lush ferns. Of course, the fact that my two youngest kids simultaneously started humming the theme song of Jurassic Park while we scoured our way through the giant ferns didn't help to quench my fantasy of this being a dinosaur island. Alas, we discovered no dinosaurs, but we did see an island so lush and beautiful that it took our breath away.

I recommend that you do this walk during summer or spring, and make sure to go on a dry day. There are parts of the walk that can and will wash away with rain and seeing as a good part of the walk is done on a narrow path on the edge of cliffs, it's important you stay safe. If you do this walk in summer, make sure to visit The Larch Box. It's just down the road from the distillery and it offers delicious food (I also tested the coffee; it is really good).

There are many lovely walks on Raasay, and if you plan on staying on the island, you should definitely try them all.

At Hallaig Road, you can find a small parking area where you can park for free. Walk up the road and soon it becomes a path and you feel the busy world disappear behind you. If you look to your right, you should see the Isle of Skye and perhaps even a whale or two.

You can't really go wrong on this walk, just keep following the path and the turn-by-turn directions when you walk through all the nooks and crannies.

TIP

You might see whales during your walk, if you pay close attention to the sea. But be careful and remember to stay safe at all times!

TURN BY TURN DIRECTIONS

Start from the parking area.

1. Walk further up the road; the road becomes a smaller path. Follow this path with the sea on your right side.
2. At 1.45 miles go left and follow the path into a wood-like area where the path leads you towards the right. Keep following the path.
3. At 1.88 miles you have reached your destination. It is a clearing: the perfect spot for a picnic, drone flying, photography, and relaxing.
4. Head back the same way.
5. At 3.77 miles you arrive at the parking area.

RAASAY DISTILLERY

Raasay Distillery is a brand-new distillery with a spectacular view. It is the first legal distillery on the island in 150 years. They started distilling in 2017 and their single malt whisky was only ready in 2020, but whenever you visit there is plenty of whisky (and even gin) for you to taste on their distillery tour. Choose between the "Distillery Tour" and the "Whisky & Chocolate Tour". Booking is required online on their website; if you have any questions send an email or give a call and the team will be happy to help.

As a special treat, you might want to consider staying at the distillery. They offer accommodation in the Borodale House which is a villa incorporated with the distillery. This definitely makes for a special distillery visit, and it's always nice not to have to worry about who's driving after a whisky tasting tour…

DRIVING DIRECTIONS

In order to reach Raasay you need to catch a ferry from the Isle of Skye. The CalMac ferry in Sconser takes you across within 25 minutes. You can check the timetables on their website.

To get from the distillery to the parking at the beginning of the walk drive south along the coast, turn right at Inverarish Terrace, and follow that road as long as possible until you reach a tiny parking area at Hallaig Road.

PRACTICAL INFORMATION

DISTILLERY / WHISKY BAR
ISLE OF RAASAY DISTILLERY
Borodale House
Isle of Raasay
Kyle, IV40 8PB
+44 (0) 1478 470178
info@raasaydistillery.com
www.raasaydistillery.com

RESTAURANT / CAFÉ
THE LARCH BOX
Tigh-an-Achaidh
Isle of Raasay
Kyle, IV40 8PB
thelarchbox@gmail.com
www.facebook.com/thelarchbox

MORE INFORMATION ABOUT THE AREA
www.raasay.com

ACCOMMODATION OPTION
ISLE OF RAASAY DISTILLERY
(see information above)

FERRY
www.calmac.co.uk

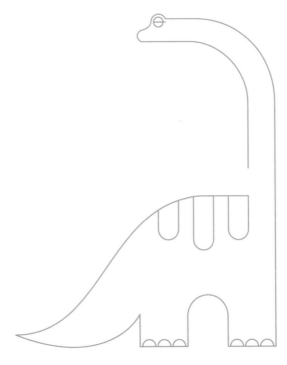

FAIRY GLEN

WE ALL NEED A BIT OF FAIRY DUST SOMETIMES.

▷ START AND END POINT

UIG HOTEL

✕ DESTINATION

THE FAIRY GLEN

🏷 WHISKY

POIT DHUBH 8 YO
BLENDED MALT WHISKY

🔛 DIFFICULTY

WALKING

☆ HIGHLIGHTS

FAIRY GLEN
LANDSCAPE,
STONE CIRCLE

⊙ DURATION OF THE HIKE

1.5 HOURS
3.1 MILES (5KM)

⋀ ELEVATION GAIN

400 FEET
(122M)

ALCOHOL
43 %
CONTENT

BLENDED MALT WHISKY

👁	**GOLDEN**
👃	**PEATY, MALT**
👅	**LIGHTLY PEATY, OAK, SMOOTH**
🛢	**MIXED CASKS**

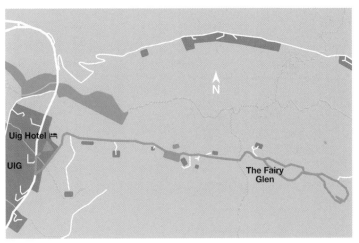

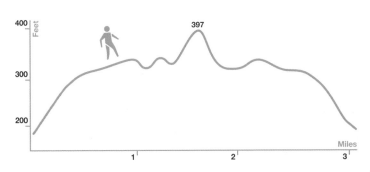

DESCRIPTION OF THE WALK

Although this is a place visited by a lot of tourists all year around, it is definitely a must-see if you are in the area. You don't have to believe in fairies to enjoy the ethereal beauty of the Fairy Glen.

This is a walk for all kinds of weather and especially beautiful at sunset and sunrise.

Park at the Uig Hotel (as the parking at the Fairy Glen can be rather crowded) and walk up the road. The hotel is nearby and so you can easily do a whisky tasting both before and after the walk. When you reach the Fairy Glen, it doesn't look like it does on the pictures in the guidebooks, but that's because you need to walk past the little lake, around the hill, and up the path. There you will see the stone spiral pictured in all photos. Up close, the stone spiral can be a bit disappointing, but if you climb the hill you will have a much better and more picturesque view of it. The surrounding area with its trees and bushes creates a wonderful fairy-tale ambiance, much more so than the spiral itself, so make sure you explore every bit of the place while you are there.

When you have explored everything to your heart's content, walk back down to the hotel and enjoy the feeling that you won't be stuck in one of those big tourist buses for hours. No, you will be sitting comfortably at the Uig Hotel with good food and drink. Sláinte!

DID YOU KNOW?

The word *uig* comes from *vík* or *úige*, meaning "Bay" in Old Norse.

TURN BY TURN DIRECTIONS

Start from parking at the Uig Hotel.

1. Walk left along the road.
2. At 0.07 miles go left and up the road.
3. At 1.43 miles turn right.
4. At 1.54 miles walk up towards Castle Ewan.
5. Go back and at 1.61 miles turn right.
6. At 1.77 miles you are back at the road. Walk left.
7. At 3.03 miles you reach the big road. Turn right.
8. At 3.11 miles you are back at the Uig Hotel.

UIG HOTEL

On the hillside above Uig Bay, just on the road to the Ferry Port, you can find the Uig Hotel. It is an old coaching inn from the 18th century with lots of charm and, lucky for us, lots of whisky. It's owned by Billy and Anne Harley, and they run it together with their very friendly team. Any questions you have about whisky, just ask Billy and he is happy to help you. The food and ale are brilliant and they have eleven bedrooms at the hotel if you want to make this your base while touring Skye.

The whisky I chose for this walk is a blended malt recommended by Billy and it was brilliant, just the thing after a very wet and cold day of walking. But there are plenty of whiskies to choose from, just take your pick.

DRIVING DIRECTIONS

You find the Uig Hotel on the A87 road headed towards the ferry for Tarbert.

PRACTICAL INFORMATION

DISTILLERY / WHISKY BAR
UIG HOTEL
Uig
Isle of Skye, IV51 9YE
+44 (0) 1470 542205
www.uig-hotel-skye.com

RESTAURANT / CAFÉ
THE UIG HOTEL
(see information above)

MORE INFORMATION ABOUT THE AREA
www.isleofskye.com

ACCOMMODATION OPTION
THE UIG HOTEL
(see information above)

ISLE OF HARRIS

THE VERY BEST OF ISLE OF HARRIS.

▷ START AND END POINT	✕ DESTINATION
PARKING AREA	**THE NORTH HARRIS EAGLE OBSERVATORY**

◇ WHISKY	▦ DIFFICULTY
ISLE OF HARRIS GIN	**WALKING**

☆ HIGHLIGHTS	◷ DURATION OF THE HIKE
EAGLES (IF YOU ARE LUCKY)	**1.25 HOURS 3.3 MILES** (5.3KM)
	△ ELEVATION GAIN
	170 FEET (52M)

GIN

ALCOHOL **45 %** CONTENT

CLEAR

JUNIPER, CITRUS, BITTER ORANGE

CITRUS, LIQUORICE, JUNIPER

NONE

ISLE OF
HARRIS
GIN

INFUSED WITH
SUGAR KELP
FROM THE OUTER HEBRIDES

45%VOL PRODUCT OF SCOTLAND 70cl e

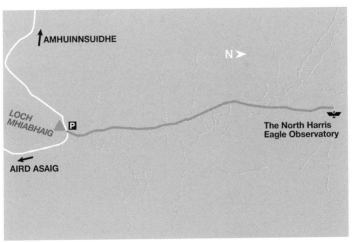

↑ AMHUINNSUIDHE

N ➤

LOCH
MHIABHAIG

P

The North Harris
Eagle Observatory

← AIRD ASAIG

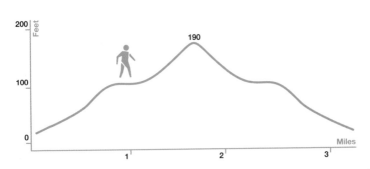

DESCRIPTION OF THE WALK

This is one of the few walks where I actually prefer it to be cloudy or even cold and snowing, as the wide and open area can become scorching hot during a sunny summer day. But then it is best not to complain about the sun, as it rarely shines when you want it to.

This walk is not a long one; if you want a longer walk there is an easy possibility to prolong it (20 km). If you are up for that, just continue past the eagle observatory. We didn't do that as there were eagles flying above us when we reached the observatory and we ended up spending several hours looking at the sky, admiring the majestic creatures.

There is a café at the distillery, but we predicted that this trip would take some time and brought lunch with us. The observatory provides shelter and benches for you to sit on, so we had a quiet picnic under the eagles.

If the weather is hot and sunny (and you don't spend all your time under the eagles) you can drive to Hushinish Beach; it's approximately 20 minutes' drive from the eagle observatory and it is an absolutely stunning beach, with turquoise clear water, white soft sand, not too many tourists. I could easily have stayed there forever (or at least as long as the sun was out).

DID YOU KNOW?

For gin to be legally labelled a gin, juniper berries need to be the predominant botanical in it. There are nine botanicals in the Harris Gin: juniper, coriander seeds, cassia bark, angelica root, bitter orange, cubeb, liquorice root, orris root, and sugar.

TURN BY TURN DIRECTIONS

Start from the parking area.

1. Walk up the path towards the North Harris Eagle Observatory.
2. At 1.63 miles you arrive at the observatory.
3. Walk back the same way.
4. At 3.26 miles you arrive back at the parking area.

HARRIS DISTILLERY

The newly opened distillery on Harris has brought new life to the island. When it opened in 2015 they had a team of ten, and when I visited the number had increased to about forty. More tourists are slowly finding their way to the beautiful island. The single malt whisky of Harris Distillery is still maturing. The goal is not to rush it but to wait for the right moment to bottle it – when that will be is anyone's guess. Until then, visitors can find solace in the Harris Gin with its decadent maritime bottle that shows the coordinates of the distillery – so you can always find your way back. To book a tour, send them an email or give them a call. Children from the age of 5 years are welcome.

If you don't want to bring a picnic on the walk, the distillery has an excellent café with local food and drinks.

DRIVING DIRECTIONS

From the distillery, drive off A868 and up to A859 and take a right turn, then a left turn at A887 and reach the parking at the eagle observatory.

To get to the Isle of Harris you need to book tickets for the ferry, and do not wait until the last minute. I did that and ended up being delayed by a day on my tour. Check the timetable and book online.

PRACTICAL INFORMATION

DISTILLERY / WHISKY BAR
ISLE OF HARRIS DISTILLERY
Tarbert
Isle of Harris, HS3 3DJ
+44 (0) 1859 502212
info@harrisdistillery.com
www.harrisdistillery.com

RESTAURANT / CAFÉ
Bring a picnic or eat at the distillery café.

MORE INFORMATION ABOUT THE AREA
www.explore-harris.com

ACCOMMODATION OPTION
ARDHASAIG HOUSE
Isle of Harris, HS3 3AJ
Tel +44 (0) 1859 502500
Mobile +44 (0) 7765 211375
accommodation@ardhasaig.co.uk
www.ardhasaig.co.uk

FERRY
www.calmac.co.uk/article/2097/Harris

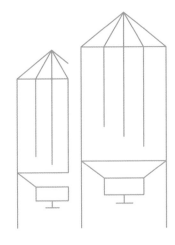

ISLE OF LEWIS

THE PERFECT BEACH FOR FAMILY OUTINGS.

▷ START AND END POINT

ARDROIL CARAVAN PARKING

✕ DESTINATION

ARDROIL BEACH

🏷 WHISKY

ABHAINN DEARG X

▦ DIFFICULTY

WALKING

☆ HIGHLIGHTS

THE BEACH

🕐 DURATION OF THE HIKE

0.75 HOUR
1.5 MILES (2.4KM)

⋀ ELEVATION GAIN

85 FEET
(26M)

ALCOHOL 46 % CONTENT

SINGLE MALT

GOLDEN

NUTMEG, FRUIT

CHOCOLATE, MALT, PEAT

OAK

ABHAINN DEARG
SINGLE MALT SCOTCH WHISKY

PRODUCED BY THE ONLY OUTER HEBRIDEAN DISTILLERY

Abhainn Distillery
Carnish Isle of
Outer Hebrides, HS
Carnish Isle of Lewis
www.abhainn

Lorem Ipsum Dolor
Carnish
Out
sle of Lewis
Lorem Ipsum

MADE IN SCOTLAND

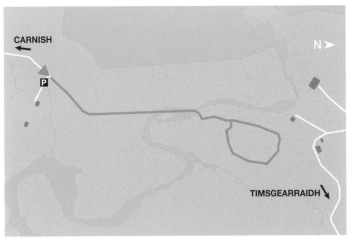

CARNISH

N

P

TIMSGEARRAIDH

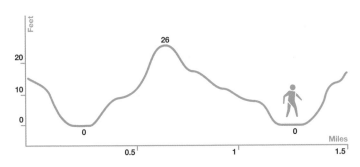

Feet

26

20

10

0

0

0

0.5

1

1.5

Miles

DESCRIPTION OF THE WALK

The beach, even when cold and grey, oozes happiness. It's a place where you can bring the whole family and create lots of happy memories that you will cherish. One could probably stay on the beach the whole day … one did not. Because just off the beach I saw something that looked like a path heading away from the beach. I looked at my family, they looked at me, and we said "what the heck, we might as well try", and so we soon walked along a path that was obviously more frequented by sheep than people. But it was just a small diversion and, soon enough, we ended up back on the beach, where you can spend hours and hours.

The beach is not too far from the distillery, but it's better to drive. Park at the caravan parking and head down to the beach. You can cross the beach and walk long and far on the sand. Follow the turn-by-turn directions and eventually you get to the tiny detour that leads you around a small hill. The ground on this detour is filled with holes and water-filled cracks. I'm not kidding, it looks like something taken out of a sci-fi book. Proceed carefully so you don't fall into the holes and cracks. Before you know it, you are walking towards the beach again. Stay and enjoy it some more or head to the distillery for a warming dram.

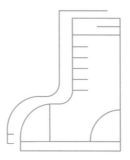

By US law, bourbon barrels are only allowed to be used once. Luckily, that means that distilleries in Scotland and other countries can buy these used barrels and utilise them for whisky.

TURN BY TURN DIRECTIONS

Start at Ardroil caravan parking.

1. Follow path towards the beach.
2. After 0.12 miles walk onto the beach.
3. Head towards the bridge.
4. At 0.44 miles you reach the bridge. Cross it and walk up the path and follow it up and to the left.
5. At 0.70 miles follow the path right around the small hill past the gate on the left. Continue forward.
6. Follow the shallow path around the hill.
7. At 0.96 miles you return to the path.
8. At 1.06 miles you return to the bridge.
9. Go back the same way you came, and cross the beach.
10. At 1.50 miles you arrive back at your starting point.

ABHAINN DEARG DISTILLERY

This distillery is one of a kind and simply a must-see if you like small, independent "do-it-yourself" distilleries. Everything about this place is so unpretentious and down to earth that you feel at ease the second you arrive. The whole whisky-making process is done the old-fashioned way; when we arrived, our guide was filling and labelling all the bottles by hand while explaining different things about the distillery to us. Kids are welcome; they can play with the cats that leisurely stroll around the distillery while you get to see everything. If you are a party of ten or more send an email to book a tour, otherwise you can check their website what time their tours are and just show up. Simply brilliant!

DRIVING DIRECTIONS

You find the distillery on B8011 on the Isle of Lewis.

PRACTICAL INFORMATION

DISTILLERY / WHISKY BAR
ABHAINN DEARG DISTILLERY
Carnish
Isle of Lewis, HS2 9EX
+44 (0) 1851 672429
enquiries@abhainndearg.co.uk
www.abhainndearg.co.uk

RESTAURANT / CAFÉ
Bring a picnic.

MORE INFORMATION ABOUT THE AREA
www.visitouterhebrides.co.uk

ACCOMMODATION OPTION
ARDHASAIG HOUSE
Isle of Harris, HS3 3AJ
Tel +44 (0)1859 50 2500
Mobile +44 (0) 7765 211375
accommodation@ardhasaig.co.uk
www.ardhasaig.co.uk

GLENBORRODALE

A WALK THROUGH A WONDERFUL NATURE RESERVE.

▷ START AND END POINT

GLENBORRODALE NATURE RESERVE PARKING

✕ DESTINATION

GLENBORRODALE NATURE RESERVE

🏷 SPIRIT

ARDNAMURCHAN
2 YO

🔡 DIFFICULTY

WALKING

☆ HIGHLIGHTS

VIEW FROM THE HILL, 200 DIFFERENT KINDS OF MOSS

◷ DURATION OF THE HIKE

1 HOUR
1.7 MILES (2.7KM)

⌃ ELEVATION GAIN

244 FEET
(105M)

ALCOHOL
54.3%
CONTENT

SPIRIT

WAREHOUSE RELEASE
LIMITED BATCH

SELECTED & BOTTLED BY
ADELPHI DISTILLERY LIMITED, ARDNAMURCHAN.
NATURAL COLOUR. UNCHILL-FILTERED.

FROM:	ARDNAMURCHAN	
BATCH NO: 9	CASK TYPE:	OLOROSO OCTAVES
AGE: 2yo	BOTTLED:	10/07/19
NO. OF BOTTLES:	159	
VOL: 54.3%		70CL

👁	**AMBER**
👃	**SLIGHTLY PEATY, SPICY**
👅	**SPICY, SMOOTH, PEATY**
🛢	**OLOROSO SHERRY, OCTAVES**

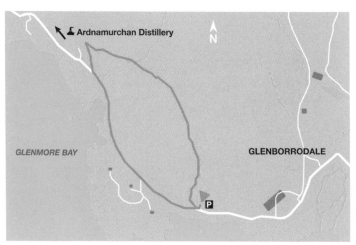

Ardnamurchan Distillery

N

GLENMORE BAY

GLENBORRODALE

P

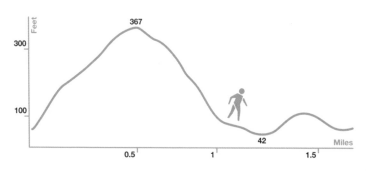

Feet

367

300

100

0.5   1   42   1.5

Miles

DESCRIPTION OF THE WALK

This is one of the walks I wish I could do again. I am very fond of being out and about in nature, and forests are my favourite place to be. And a forest that contains more than 200 species of moss is just too fascinating to pass. And for bird enthusiasts, this place is simply heaven.

However, when I did this walk it was with my youngest son. Instead of stopping and looking at the mosses and ferns, we raced up the hill and held a contest to see who was most out of breath. And after that, our focus was finding our way along the path. I tend to get lost from time to time, even on easy walks (which is why I often bring my husband. Please don't tell him I said so, he believes I take him with me for his charming company.)
But we did enjoy the lush forest and it was thrilling to walk through it.
Next time, I'll have to do a slower tour of the area to appreciate it more.

From the parking lot walk up to the road, and just a few feet to the right you find a small path up to the right. Follow the path and the turn-by-turn directions and head up to the top of the hill to savour the glorious view. Head on along the path. In several places there will be small wooden bridges that you need to cross, but they are on the trail so you can't get lost. Follow the trail until you reach the road and then head back to the parking lot along the road.

If you have time to spare, you should stroll along the coastline as well, perhaps you can spot an otter or a seal.

=== TIP ===

Bring your binoculars on this trip, there are a lot of fascinating birds to spot, including a Golden Eagle.

TURN BY TURN DIRECTIONS

Park two miles (a bit more than 3 kilometers) from the distillery at Glenborrodale Nature Reserve parking lot.

1. Walk 0.03 miles right from the parking lot and up to the trail.
2. At 0.55 miles you reach the top. Continue onwards on the Glenborrodale footpath.
3. At 0.96 miles you reach the main road.
4. Turn left and walk back to the parking area.
5. At 1.67 miles you have returned to the parking lot.

ARDNAMURCHAN DISTILLERY

Ardnamurchan Distillery is a new addition to the Adelphi bottling company. It is newly opened and is situated on the lush peninsula of Ardnamurchan. It lies well-hidden along a small single-track road. Ardnamurchan coexists with nature; it does not hide on purpose. Even though it might not be the easiest distillery to find, it is worth looking for it. The team is very friendly and there are several tours to choose from. Make sure to book in advance.

They even have a very special feature: If you have always dreamt of owning your own personal cask, you can email them and ask if that is possible.

DID YOU KNOW?

It takes three years and one day for a whisky to legally become a whisky. Although this spirit looks like whisky and tastes like whisky it is still called "spirit". It tastes marvellous!

DRIVING DIRECTIONS

The distillery is situated close to the town of Glenbeg off the B8007 road.

PRACTICAL INFORMATION

DISTILLERY / WHISKY BAR
ARDNAMURCHAN DISTILLERY LTD
Glenbeg
Argyll, PH36 4JG
+44 (0) 1972 500285
ardnamurchan@adelphidistillery.com
www.adelphidistillery.com

RESTAURANT / CAFÉ
Bring a picnic.
If you are staying at Kilcamb Lodge (see
Accommodation option) you can order a lunch
pack the evening before. It's delicious.

MORE INFORMATION ABOUT THE AREA
www.rspb.org.uk

ACCOMMODATION OPTION
KILCAMB LODGE HOTEL
Strontian
Argyll, PH36 4HY
+44 (0) 1967 402257
enquiries@kilcamblodge.co.uk
www.kilcamblodge.co.uk

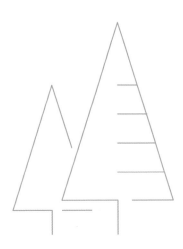

NC'NEAN

A LONG WALK WITH A GLORIOUS VIEW.

▷ START AND END POINT

NC'NEAN DISTILLERY

✕ DESTINATION

THE END OF THE ROAD

◇ SPIRIT

NC'NEAN ORGANIC SINGLE MALT SCOTCH WHISKY

卍 DIFFICULTY

WALKING

☆ HIGHLIGHTS

COFFEE AND CAKE AT THE END OF THE WALK, VIEW OF THE SEA, LOCH NA DROMA BUIDHE

◷ DURATION OF THE HIKE

4 HOURS 10 MILES (16KM)

⌃ ELEVATION GAIN

1118 FEET (314M)

ORGANIC
SINGLE MALT

 LIGHT AMBER

SPICE AND OAK

 SPICE, PEACH,
LEMON POSSET

 RED WINE
AND AMERICAN
WHISKY BARRELS

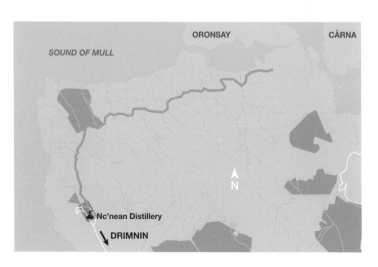

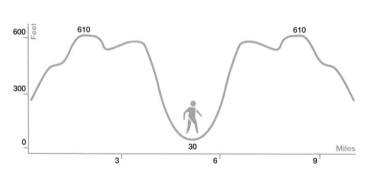

DESCRIPTION OF THE WALK

This is a long walk, and will feel twice as long if it rains. There is no shelter along the path so if it pours down prepare to become very wet. If you go during a sunny day, this is an amazing walk.

There are parts where you can walk leisurely while talking, and parts where you can admire nature and wildlife. And then there are amazing viewpoints that leave you breathless as you observe the staggering beauty around you.

Park at the parking lot at the distillery and let the staff know that you are there and heading out. Follow the turn-by-turn directions. There isn't another path so you can't get lost, just keep on walking.

Along the way, you can find several spots that are great for a picnic so remember to bring that lunch with you, along with lots and lots of water to drink (no, whisky doesn't count, or so I was told repeatedly by my family on this walk). Enjoy the trip, and when you return to the distillery you will be greeted with open arms – and cake and coffee or tea.

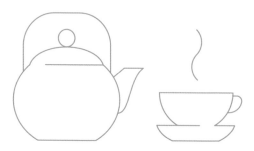

The name Nc'nean was inspired by the ancient Gaelic goddess Neachneohain. She is the queen of spirits and protector of nature, a strong and independent deity who is never afraid of walking her own path. If you get lost during one of your walks you know which goddess to pray to.

TURN BY TURN DIRECTIONS

Start at the distillery parking lot.

1. Walk back up to the road.
2. At 0.14 miles you reach the road. Turn left.
3. Continue the path.
4. At 0.39 miles walk through the gate and continue.
5. At 1.73 miles walk through another gate.
6. At 3.70 miles walk through yet another gate.
7. At 3.75 miles you reach a viewpoint. This is a great photo opportunity.
8. At 4.62 miles you cross a river. Continue ahead.
9. At 5.20 miles you reach the end point.
10. Return the same way.
11. At 9.94 miles you reach the distillery again.

NC'NEAN DISTILLERY

This distillery is simply a must visit – and no, I am not only saying this because there is coffee and cake on their tours, even though this is a big plus for me. No, it's the drive of the team, the passion, the interest they all have in creating something spectacular, and the constant striving for new recipes and new methods. It is an inspiring place to visit. You can feel the energy buzzing when you are there.

Their organic whisky was not quite ready when I visited last, but I have been lucky enough to taste in since, and it did not let me down. Light, smooth, and elegant are the keywords to describe this whisky. I can also highly recommend their triple-distilled botanical spirit. It is amazing.

Book your tour in advance, and if you have any questions, the staff will be very happy to help you.

DRIVING DIRECTIONS

The distillery is situated north-west from Fiunary on B849.

PRACTICAL INFORMATION

DISTILLERY / WHISKY BAR
NC'NEAN DISTILLERY
Drimnin
By Lochaline, PA80 5XZ
+44 (0) 1967 421698
hello@ncnean.com
www.ncnean.com

RESTAURANT / CAFÉ
Bring a picnic.
If you are staying at Kilcamb Lodge (see
Accommodation option) you can order a lunch
pack the evening before. It's delicious.

MORE INFORMATION ABOUT THE AREA
www.ardnamurchan.com

ACCOMMODATION OPTION
KILCAMB LODGE HOTEL
Strontian
Argyll, PH36 4HY
+44 (0) 1967 402257
enquiries@kilcamblodge.co.uk
www.kilcamblodge.co.uk

KILMARTIN

A LOVELY HISTORIC WALK.

▷ START AND END POINT

KILMARTIN HOTEL

✕ DESTINATION

CAIRN STONES

🏷 SPIRIT

COPPER DOG BLENDED MALT

🔳 DIFFICULTY

WALKING

☆ HIGHLIGHTS

CAIRNS, VIEW OF KILMARTIN GLEN, LAPIDARIUM, TEMPLE WOOD STANDING STONES

◷ DURATION OF THE HIKE

1.5 HOURS 3 MILES (5KM)

△ ELEVATION GAIN

210 FEET (64M)

SPEYSIDE BLENDED MALT

ALCOHOL **40 %** CONTENT

👁	LIGHT GOLD
👃	PEAR, HONEY, APPLES
👅	ORANGE PEEL, CHOCOLATE, SPICE
🛢	EIGHT DIFFERENT SINGLEMALT BLENDS FROM SPEYSIDE

EST. 1893
THE CRAIGELLACHIE HOTEL SCOTLAND
COPPER DOG
SPEYSIDE BLENDED MALT SCOTCH WHISKY
BLEND: Copper Dog   BLENDER:
MARRIED IN: Speyside   BATCH NO: 16/0673
ALCOHOL: 40% vol   VOLUME: 700 ml
– PRODUCT OF SCOTLAND –

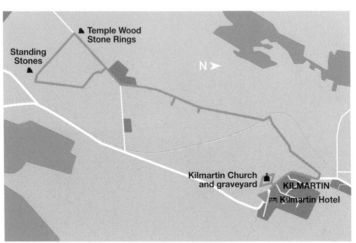

Temple Wood Stone Rings

Standing Stones

N ➤

Kilmartin Church and graveyard

KILMARTIN

Kilmartin Hotel

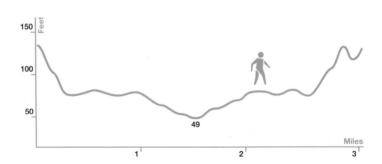

DESCRIPTION OF THE WALK

Get to know the history of this exciting area. You will see prehistoric stone circles, man-made piles of stones called cairns, a graveyard, and a church along your way. The scenery is amazing and the ambiance is tranquil.

Park at the Kilmartin Hotel. Follow the turn-by-turn directions and you can see several cairns on your way.

In this area you can fly a drone which will give you fantastic photos, but please check the rules beforehand just to be on the safe side. The walk can be done in all kinds of weather so there is nothing to keep you back.

If you like you can bring a lunch pack with you; if the weather permits it there are plenty of opportunities for you to enjoy a lunch out in the open. You can also head back to the hotel and enjoy a hearty meal there.

A "Copper Dog" is a piece of equipment used at distilleries to extract whisky from the cask for sampling.

TURN BY TURN DIRECTIONS

Start at the Kilmartin Hotel.

1. Cross the road, and go right.
2. At 0.19 miles turn left and take the path through the gate.
3. At 0.34 miles you reach Glebe Cairn. Continue on the path forward.
4. At 0.47 miles cross the bridge and go left.
5. At 0.72 miles you reach North Cairn. Continue along the path.
6. At 0.84 miles you arrive at Middle Cairn. Walk back to the path again and continue your way.
7. At 1.09 miles go right and down the road.
8. At 1.17 miles you reach South Cairn. Continue along the path.
9. At 1.45 miles go right and to the Standing Stones. Continue on the path to the road.
10. Cross the road to reach Temple Wood Stone Circle.
11. Go left up the road.
12. At 1.19 miles go left and down the path.
13. At 2.43 miles cross the bridge again.
14. Follow the path up to the road.
15. At 2.71 miles go right.
16. At 2.89 miles go right into the churchyard.
17. At 2.94 miles you reach the Lapidarium. Continue through the churchyard.
18. At 3.00 miles walk through the gate and up to the road and to the hotel.
19. You arrive at the hotel at 3.06 miles.

KILMARTIN HOTEL

I spent an entire evening observing and interviewing the team working at Kilmartin, and what a delight it was. It felt like I got a peek behind the curtains, and what I saw made me want to come back again. The food and of course the choice of whiskies were absolutely brilliant. And a place where the boss makes sure that everyone in his team gets home safely after work at night – that is a place I like. Don't let the facade fool you, the rooms might not be extravagant but they are clean, and the food is excellent. It is one of those places you want to come back to. It is a down-to-earth hotel where the locals as well as tourists gather to have a pint, whisky, or gin and tonic. If you don't find the whisky you are looking for, talk to the owner. He changes the whisky selection often and is more than happy to listen to any requests or questions regarding whisky.

DRIVING DIRECTIONS

Kilmartin Hotel is just north on the Oban road on the A816.

PRACTICAL INFORMATION

DISTILLERY / WHISKY BAR
KILMARTIN HOTEL
Kilmartin
Argyll, PA31 8RQ
+44 (0) 1546 510250
info@kilmartin-hotel.com
www.kilmartin-hotel.com

RESTAURANT / CAFÉ
KILMARTIN HOTEL
(see information above)

MORE INFORMATION ABOUT THE AREA
www.kilmartin-hotel.com

ACCOMMODATION OPTION
KILMARTIN HOTEL
(see information above)

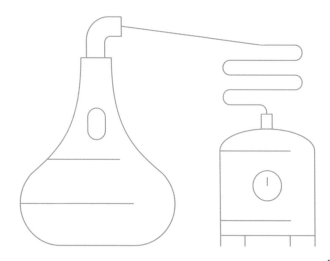

LOCH STAOISHA

A WILD NATURE WALK.

▷ START AND END POINT	✗ DESTINATION
ARDNAHOE DISTILLERY	**LOCH STAOISHA**

🏷 WHISKY	🔲 DIFFICULTY
HEPBURN'S CHOICE 2009	**WALKING**

☆ HIGHLIGHTS	⊙ DURATION OF THE HIKE
ARDNAHOE LOCH LOCH STAOISHA	**1 HOUR 3 MILES** (4.9KM)
	△ ELEVATION GAIN
	170 FEET (88M)

SINGLE MALT

ALCOHOL 46% CONTENT

👁	LIGHT GOLD
👃	MALT, HONEY, FRUIT
👅	FRUIT, HONEY, APPLES
🛢	N/A

HEPBURN'S CHOICE

SINGLE MALT SCOTCH WHISKY

DISTILLED AT

DISTILLERY 2009

AGED 7 YEARS

BOTTLED IN 2017

SINGLE CASE

PRODUCT OF SCOTLAND

BOTTLED BY LANGSIDE DISTILLERS, G3 GAX

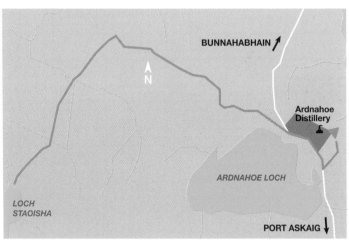

BUNNAHABHAIN

Ardnahoe Distillery

ARDNAHOE LOCH

LOCH STAOISHA

PORT ASKAIG

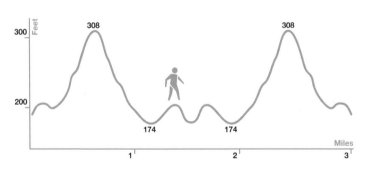

DESCRIPTION OF THE WALK

This is a great little walk to clear your head after the distillery tour. You won't have to walk for too long before you get to a path that leads you towards Loch Staoisha. It is an enjoyable walk where you meet ferns and very often puddles. There are wooden planks and stones to help you walk through watery areas, so you can always continue on your path. There may also be places where there aren't any planks, so make sure you wear waterproof boots, just to be on the safe side.

Follow the turn-by-turn directions, you can't go wrong. The distillery's café awaits you with a lunch menu and cake.

TURN BY TURN DIRECTIONS

Start from the distillery.

1. Walk right up the road.
2. At 0.29 miles go left up the path.
3. Keep following the path.
4. At 1.52 miles you have reached Loch Staoisha.
5. Walk back the same way.
6. At 3.03 miles you arrive at the distillery again.

ARDNAHOE DISTILLERY

Ardnahoe is one of the newer distilleries in Scotland and their first distillation began in 2018, so their first whisky might not be ready when you visit. But fear not, they offer plenty of whisky in their vast shop and there will be whisky tasting on the tours. They have several different tours to choose from, including the "Kinship Collection & Tasting" which offers a tasting of six rare Islay single malts. This tour is expensive but a once-in-a-lifetime experience for true whisky enthusiasts. If you want a smaller tour, "The Spirit of Ardnahoe" is perfect and you get to take your tasting glass home with you. Get in touch with them and they will help you book the perfect tour for you.

The visitor centre has a restaurant where you can have lunch or just cake and coffee.

DRIVING DIRECTIONS

The distillery is close to Port Askaig. To get to Islay you need to take the ferry to Port Askaig. Remember to check ferry times in time.

PRACTICAL INFORMATION

DISTILLERY / WHISKY BAR
ARDNAHOE
Port Askaig
Isle of Islay
Argyll, PA46 7RN
+44 (0) 1496 840777
info@ardnahoedistillery.com
www.ardnahoedistillery.com

RESTAURANT / CAFÉ
THE ARDNAHOE DISTILLERY
(see information above)

MORE INFORMATION ABOUT THE AREA
www.islayinfo.com

ACCOMMODATION OPTION
BALLYGRANT INN & RESTAURANT
Ballygrant
Isle of Islay
Argyll, PA45 7QR
+44 (0) 1496 840277
info@ballygrant-inn.co.uk
www.ballygrant-inn.com

FERRY
www.calmac.co.uk

LOCH BALLYGRANT

THE PERFECT COUNTRY WALK.

▷ START AND END POINT

BALLYGRANT INN

✕ DESTINATION

LOCH BALLYGRANT

🔖 WHISKY

BRUICHLADDICH
10 YO

🔳 DIFFICULTY

WALKING

☆ HIGHLIGHTS

LOCH BALLYGRANT, WOODLAND

🕐 DURATION OF THE HIKE

2.5 HOURS
6.2 MILES (10KM)

⌂ ELEVATION GAIN

377 FEET
(115M)

SINGLE MALT

GOLD

FRUIT, PEACH, CHOCOLATE

SULTANAS, CHOCOLATE, HONEY

BOURBON AND SHERRY

ALCOHOL **46 %** CONTENT

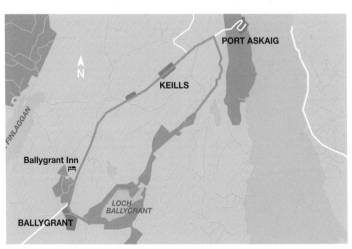

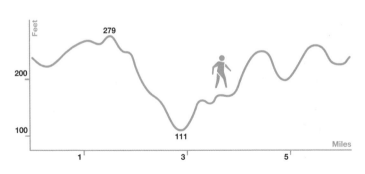

DESCRIPTION OF THE WALK

An enjoyable walk along the countryside through woodland and along a beautiful loch, this is the perfect way to spend an afternoon.

Start from the Ballygrant Inn, follow the road and the turn-by-turn directions and you will soon come to a woodland area where the loch is. Walk along it and follow the path further along the woods. Close to the loch there is a picnic area where you can stop for lunch. Continue on your walk; it takes you back to Ballygrant.

The path stops and ends a couple of times. If you can, cross the road and walk on the sidewalk as described in the turn-by-turn directions. The walk is just short of 10 km and it's nice in all kinds of weather.

TURN BY TURN DIRECTIONS

1. Cross the road from Ballygrant and follow the path to the right.
2. At 0.32 miles follow the road along the houses.
3. At 0.37 miles go left up the road.
4. At 0.67 miles turn left down a private road.
5. At 0.73 miles go left and walk past the farm shed and follow the road ahead.
6. At 0.87 miles you reach the loch. Turn left.
7. There is a picnic area on your right. This is a good place for lunch.
8. Follow the path.
9. At 3.13 miles turn left.
10. At 3.29 miles go left and through the steel gate. Continue forward.
11. At 3.61 miles go left and follow the path.
12. At 4.17 miles you reach a town. Cross the road and walk on the sidewalk.
13. At 4.42 miles cross the road again and continue on the footpath.
14. At 6.08 miles cross the road once more.
15. At 6.17 miles you have returned to your starting point.

BALLYGRANT INN

If you are going to stay at an inn, it is always a great advantage when it has an award-winning whisky bar. The Ballygrant simply has it all: great whisky, tasty food, lovely rooms, and it's situated just outside the town of Ballygrant with its spectacular views.

There are well over 400 whiskies at their bar, so there are lots to choose from, and if you have any questions, the owners are happy to help. They also have whisky-tasting tours, so you can experience many different whiskies from all over Scotland. If you are looking for whisky tasting for larger groups, make sure to get in touch beforehand.

DRIVING DIRECTIONS

To get to Islay, you need to take the ferry to Port Askaig. The Ballygrant Inn is just off the A846.

PRACTICAL INFORMATION

DISTILLERY / WHISKY BAR
BALLYGRANT INN & RESTAURANT
Ballygrant
Isle of Islay
Argyll, PA45 7QR
+44 (0) 1496 840277
info@ballygrant-inn.co.uk
www.ballygrant-inn.com

RESTAURANT / CAFÉ
BALLYGRANT INN & RESTAURANT
(see information above)

MORE INFORMATION ABOUT THE AREA
www.islayinfo.com

ACCOMMODATION OPTION
BALLYGRANT INN & RESTAURANT
(see information above)

FERRY
www.calmac.co.uk

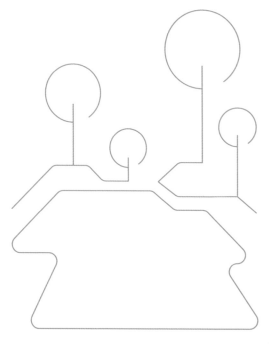

MACHIR BAY

BEAUTIFUL SANDY BEACH WITH STUNNING SUNSETS.

▷ START AND END POINT

KILCHOMAN DISTILLERY

✕ DESTINATION

MACHIR BAY

🏷 WHISKY

MACHIR BAY SINGLE MALT

▦ DIFFICULTY

WALKING

☆ HIGHLIGHTS

THE BEACH

⊙ DURATION OF THE HIKE

2 HOURS
4.5 MILES (7.3KM)

⋀ ELEVATION GAIN

177 FEET
(54M)

ALCOHOL
46 %
CONTENT

SINGLE MALT

 GOLDEN

 LEMON, VANILLA, PEACH

 BUTTERSCOTCH, SULTANAS, SMOKE

BOURBON AND SHERRY

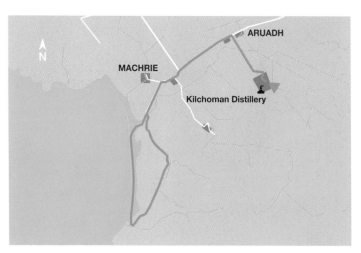

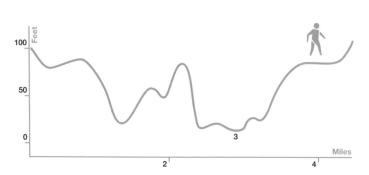

DESCRIPTION OF THE WALK

I recommend going on the distillery tour first and then doing the walk after. Either bring a driver's dram with you, or buy a bottle of the Machir Bay single malt and enjoy it on the beach of Machir Bay: It is only fitting to drink this whisky on the beautiful sandy beach that it is named after.

Walk or drive from the distillery towards the beach and take the path left at the beginning of the parking area. It's a fairly big parking area and it's possible to park even if you are driving a camper.

You can do the walk in all kinds of weather but it is of course nicest when the sun is out. If it's warm you can even go for a dip in the sea.

Follow the turn-by-turn directions along the path to, from, and along the beach and when you are done, head back towards the distillery where you can have refreshments either inside the café or outside in the courtyard.

========== TIP ==========

If you like your whisky slightly peaty but want to avoid the taste of a wild bonfire, look for whiskies with a PPM below 20. PPM means "(phenol) parts per million", and heavily peated whiskies are above 30 PPM.

TURN BY TURN DIRECTIONS

Start from the distillery.

1. Walk up to the main road and go left.
2. At 0.93 miles walk straight ahead.
3. At 1.35 miles you reach the beginning of the parking area for the beach. Go left and follow the path.
4. At 2.32 miles go left through the gate, and follow the path to the beach.
5. Walk along the beach.
6. At 3.03 miles look for a path on the right.
7. At 3.08 miles take the path to the right off the beach.
8. Walk back to the parking lot.
9. At 3.17 miles you reach the parking area.
10. Walk to the road and walk back to the distillery the same way you came.
11. At 4.54 miles you arrive at the distillery.

KILCHOMAN DISTILLERY

As an independent distillery, Kilchoman is one of the few that handles the entire process of whisky making themselves. They have their own barley fields, they malt the barley themselves, they handle the peating process, and they mature and bottle the whisky.

It is a charming distillery and a joy to visit. They have several different tours to choose from. Just go to their website and book the tour online.

After the tour you can enjoy lunch at their café and browse around in their vast gift shop.

For those driving, they offer driver's drams to take with you. Those who drink whisky will get a little whisky glass on the tour to take home afterwards.

DRIVING DIRECTIONS

You can find the distillery just off B8018 on Islay. To get to Islay you need to take the ferry to Port Askaig.

PRACTICAL INFORMATION

DISTILLERY / WHISKY BAR
KILCHOMAN DISTILLERY
Rockside Farm
Isle of Islay
Argyll, PA49 7UT
+44 (0) 1496 850011
kilchomandistillery@mailmarkuk.com
www.kilchomandistillery.com

RESTAURANT / CAFÉ
KILCHOMAN DISTILLERY
(see information above)

MORE INFORMATION ABOUT THE AREA
www.islayinfo.com

ACCOMMODATION OPTION
BALLYGRANT INN & RESTAURANT
Ballygrant
Isle of Islay
Argyll, PA45 7QR
+44 (0) 1496 840277
info@ballygrant-inn.co.uk
www.ballygrant-inn.com

FERRY
www.calmac.co.uk

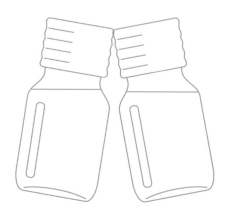

LOW ASKOMILL

TAKE A WALK ALONG THE SEASIDE.

▷ START AND END POINT

GLEN SCOTIA DISTILLERY

✕ DESTINATION

COASTLINE

🏷 WHISKY

GLEN SCOTIA 2001

▦ DIFFICULTY

WALKING

☆ HIGHLIGHTS

SEA VIEW, VIEW OF DAVAAR LIGHTHOUSE

◷ DURATION OF THE HIKE

2 HOURS
4.9 MILES (7.9KM)

△ ELEVATION GAIN

288 FEET
(88M)

SINGLE MALT

ALCOHOL 57.1% CONTENT

ESTD. 1832

GLEN SCOTIA
SINGLE MALT SCOTCH WHISKY

CASK : 560
2001
First Fill Bourbon

CLASSIC CAMPBELTOWN MALT

GLEN SCOTIA, CAMPBELTOWN

DISTILLED, MATURED
20cl & BOTTLED IN SCOTLAND 57,1%

GOLDEN

FRUIT, HONEY, OAK

SPICE, FRUIT, ORANGE PEEL

BOURBON

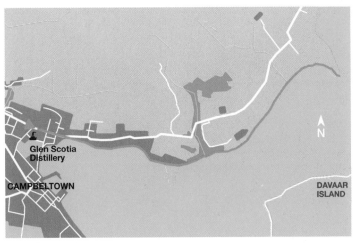

Glen Scotia Distillery

CAMPBELTOWN

DAVAAR ISLAND

N

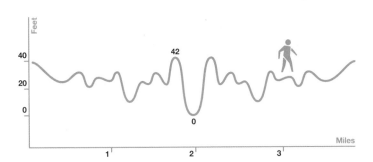

Feet

40

20

0

42

0

Miles

1   2   3

DESCRIPTION OF THE WALK

Campbeltown is always buzzing with life but even more so during summer when the seaside is busiest. After tasting a few drams, a bit of fresh sea air is just perfect, so head down High Street and continue onwards towards the seaside. Walk along Low Askomill Walk and make sure you take the path to the right.

At first the path is easy, but the further out you go, the more bushes are in your way; you'll have to make your way through them. Going head-to-head with shrubbery is worth it, for the view at the end is picturesque. At the end of the headland you have an amazing view of the sea. If you are planning on using a drone, make sure you check if it's allowed. Walk the same way back to the distillery to get to your car.

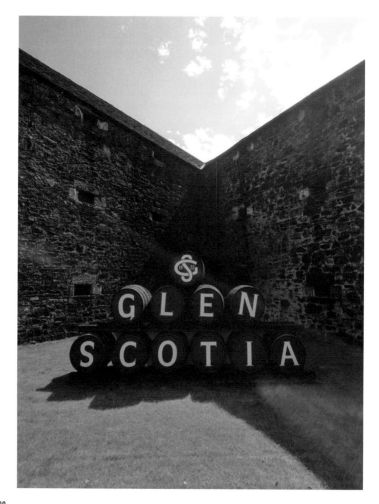

TURN BY TURN DIRECTIONS

Start from the distillery.

1. Walk right down High Street.
2. At 0.21 miles continue on Low Askomill Walk.
3. At 0.98 miles turn right.
4. Follow the path.
5. At 2.46 miles you have reached the end of the headland.
6. Use the same way to get back.
7. At 4.90 miles you return to the distillery again.

GLEN SCOTIA DISTILLERY

With most of its design dating back to the 1830s, this is one of the most charming distilleries I've visited. The team is keeping up an old tradition with their methods of distilling. They offer several different tours, all with tastings at the end. The whole place is packed with history and charm and once you start tasting the whisky you will want to stay the rest of the day and forget all about walking...

Get in contact with them to find out which tour will be best for you.

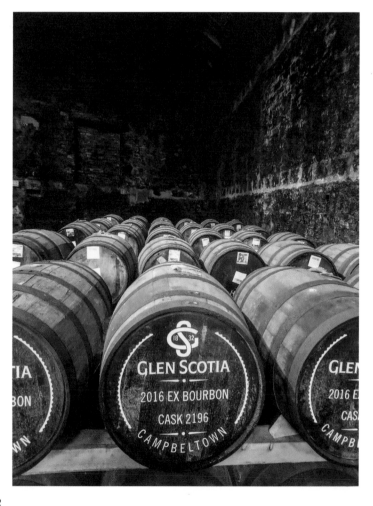

DRIVING DIRECTIONS

You can find Glen Scotia Distillery in the heart of Campbeltown.

PRACTICAL INFORMATION

DISTILLERY / WHISKY BAR
GLEN SCOTIA DISTILLERY
12 High Street
Campbeltown
Argyll, PA28 6DS
+44 (0) 1586 552288
info@lochlomondgroup.com
www.glenscotia.com/distillery

RESTAURANT / CAFÉ
ARDSHIEL HOTEL
Kilkerran Road
Campbeltown
Argyll, PA28 6JL
Tel +44 (0) 1586 552133
info@ardshiel.co.uk
reservations@ardshiel.co.uk
www.ardshiel.co.uk

MORE INFORMATION ABOUT THE AREA
www.explorecampbeltown.com

ACCOMMODATION OPTION
ARDSHIEL HOTEL
(see information above)

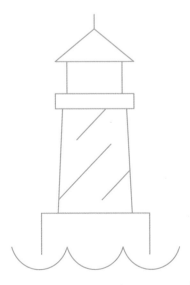

DAVAAR ISLAND

LET'S GO EXPLORE AN ISLAND!

▷ START AND END POINT	✕ DESTINATION
THE BEACH	**DAVAAR ISLAND CAVE**

⬥ WHISKY	▦ DIFFICULTY
CADENHEAD'S BENRINNES 23 YO	**WALKING**

☆ HIGHLIGHTS	◷ DURATION OF THE HIKE
DAVAAR ISLAND, THE CRUCIFIXION CAVE	**1.5 HOURS** **3 MILES** (4.9KM)
	⌃ ELEVATION GAIN
	33 FEET (10M)

ALCOHOL
53.5%
CONTENT

SINGLE MALT

CADENHEAD'S
WAREHOUSE
SINGLE MALT
SCOTCH WHISKY
TASTING

Distilled at
BENRINNES
Distillery
Distilled: 1995 Age: 23 y/o
Wood Type: Hogshead
Contents: 70cl Strength: 53.5%
Product of Scotland
WM. CADENHEAD LTD.
Campbeltown • Scotland

GOLDEN

FRUIT, MALT, OAK

ORANGE PEEL,
SPICE, HONEY

HOGSHEAD

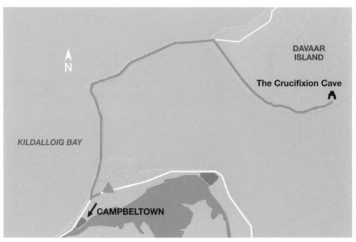

N

DAVAAR
ISLAND

The Crucifixion Cave

KILDALLOIG BAY

CAMPBELTOWN

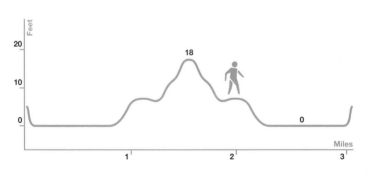

Feet

20

10

0

18

Miles

1   2   3

DESCRIPTION OF THE WALK

This is an absolutely stunning walk, one that I would love to do again and again. Just the view of Davaar Island is breathtaking.

Please be mindful of the tide before you head out. Locals often talk about tourists getting stuck on the island because they lost track of time (no, it wasn't me for once…).

Park by the side of the road close to the gate towards the island. There is room for a couple of cars only. Head out and cross the beach towards the lighthouse or along the sand where it is possible to walk.

When you reach the island, walk right and around the island. The beach on the right side is covered in rocks and big stones and it can be very slippery if it's raining, so be careful.

In the cave there is a painting of Jesus made by a local art teacher in 1887. He painted the life-size Jesus in secret which made local fishermen believe the painting was a miracle. They were sorely disappointed when they found out this was not the case. That the painting has survived all this time in a cave is a small miracle in itself. Luckily, local artists look after it to ensure it is safe.

When you are ready to leave the cave behind, walk back the same way to where you started.

It is a good idea to bring lots of water and food. The cave is a perfect place to have a rest and a picnic, but you can eat in town as well if you like. There are plenty of options.

DID YOU KNOW?

Although Campbeltown is famous for its whisky, It has a lot more to offer than that. If architecture is something that intrigues you, make sure to take a walk along the waterfront. There you will find many interesting buildings, amongst them the Wee Picture House, which was designed by Albert Gardner from the Glasgow School of Art in the early 1900s. This cinema was one of the first buildings to be specifically built for cinematic purposes in Scotland. It is a gem to behold.

TURN BY TURN DIRECTIONS

Start from the parking at Le'arside Road. There is a small parking area on the waterside.

1. At .03 miles turn right to the path towards the beach.
2. Follow the sandy path; walk towards the island.
3. At 0.45 miles you reach an old lighthouse. Continue walking towards the island.
4. At 0.92 miles you reach Davaar Island. Go right and follow the coastline.
5. At 1.52 miles you reach the cave.
6. Walk back the same way.
7. At 3.05 miles you arrive at the parking lot.

CADENHEAD'S

If you enjoy being surrounded by a lot of different whisky casks you should definitely visit Cadenhead's. They have a massive collection of whisky casks. They bottle, mature, buy, and sell whisky: it is simply whisky heaven. There are two tours at Cadenhead's, the Cadenhead Warehouse Tasting tour and the Taste It tour. The Taste It tour has six different whiskies to try out as well as the option to add a lunch platter. Book by phone, email, or via their website.

DRIVING DIRECTIONS

Cadenhead's is based at the same place as Springbank and Kilkerran in the middle of Campbeltown.

PRACTICAL INFORMATION

DISTILLERY / WHISKY BAR
CADENHEAD'S (SPRINGBANK DISTILLERY)
9 Bolgam Street
Campbeltown
Argyll, PA28 6HZ
+44 (0) 1586 554258
enquiries@cadenhead.scot
www.springbank.scot

RESTAURANT / CAFÉ
Bring a picnic.

MORE INFORMATION ABOUT THE AREA
www.explorecampbeltown.com

ACCOMMODATION OPTION
ARDSHIEL HOTEL
Kilkerran Road
Campbeltown
Argyll, PA28 6JL
Tel +44 (0) 1586 552133
info@ardshiel.co.uk
reservations@ardshiel.co.uk
www.ardshiel.co.uk

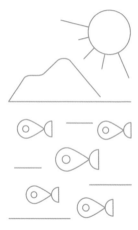

FOREST WALK

LUSH FOREST WALK. BEWARE OF THE MIDGES!

▷ START AND END POINT	✕ DESTINATION
SPRINGBANK DISTILLERY	**FOREST**
✎ WHISKY	▦ DIFFICULTY
SPRINGBANK SINGLE MALT	**WALKING**
☆ HIGHLIGHTS	◷ DURATION OF THE HIKE
CROSSHILL LOCH, WOODLAND	**2 HOURS 4.2 MILES** (6.7KM)
	△ ELEVATION GAIN
	522 FEET (159M)

ALCOHOL 53.5% CONTENT

SINGLE MALT

SPRINGBANK
Single Malt Scotch Whisky

SPRINGBANK DISTILLERY

PRIVATE BOTTLING
For
Distillery Visitors
2019

Distilled by J.A.A. SCITGHILL A CO LTD
Springbank Distillery Campbeltown Scotland
PRODUCT OF SCOTLAND

👁	LIGHT GOLDEN
👃	PEAT, GRASS, ORANGE
👄	PEAT, FRUIT, ORANGE
🛢	N/A

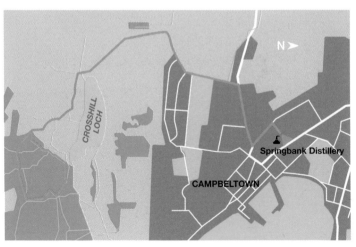

CROSSHILL LOCH

N ➤

Springbank Distillery

CAMPBELTOWN

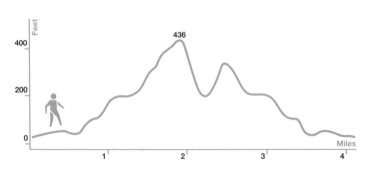

Feet

400

200

0

436

1   2   3   4

Miles

DESCRIPTION OF THE WALK

After a day in the hustle and bustle of a busy town, it is nice to go for a walk in nature and enjoy the peace and quiet.

This is a really lovely walk and can be done in all kinds of weather. However, if you do this walk during midge season make sure you have the right gear with you because they are fierce. Midge season is between May and September but check with the Scottish midge forecast to find out how bad it is when you are planning on going.

Follow the turn-by-turn directions and soon you are out of town and on your way up the hill towards the forest. It's lush and cool during summertime and absolutely stunning. Walk through the forest until you end up at the beginning of it again. Walk down towards town, passing the pasture you went by on the way up – and be careful if the bull is out!

The walk is just shy of 7 km. If you want to shorten it you can drive up to the fenced pasture and find a parking space there.

=== **DID YOU KNOW?** ===

Once there were over 30 distilleries in Campbeltown. Now there are only a few left.

TURN BY TURN DIRECTIONS

Start from the distillery parking lot.

1. Walk south-west on Well Close.
2. At 0.05 miles walk left down Glebe Street.
3. At 0.19 miles turn right at Witchburn Road.
4. At 0.46 miles turn left onto Tomaig Road.
5. At 1.04 miles walk straight ahead past a house on the right.
6. At 1.07 miles walk through the gate and follow the path up towards the woods.
7. At 1.68 miles you reach the woods. Walk on.
8. At 1.98 miles turn left down the path.
9. At 2.22 miles go left and follow the path.
10. At 2.52 miles you reach the main path. Turn right.
11. At 3.13 miles you are back at the gate.
12. Go back to the distillery the same way you came.
13. At 4.20 miles you have returned.

SPRINGBANK DISTILLERY

It's difficult to comprehend that a lively town by the seaside only has a few whisky distilleries left. Springbank is one of them and they recently opened another distillery, Kilkerran, determined to revive the distillery tradition in Campbeltown again. During summer Springbank runs a whisky school where students can become part of the production team and learn how a distillery works. The staff offers many different tours and tastings. Have a look on their website and find the tour that suits you best. Make a booking inquiry online by email, or phone. They are very friendly and always happy to help with any questions you might have about the tours.

DRIVING DIRECTIONS

Springbank Distillery is at the same place as Cadenhead's and Kilkerran in the middle of Campbeltown.

PRACTICAL INFORMATION

DISTILLERY / WHISKY BAR
SPRINGBANK
9 Bolgam Street
Campbeltown
Argyll, PA28 6HZ
+44 (0) 1586 552009
info@springbank.scot
www.springbank.scot

RESTAURANT / CAFÉ
Bring a picnic.

MORE INFORMATION ABOUT THE AREA
www.explorecampbeltown.com

ACCOMMODATION OPTION
ARDSHIEL HOTEL
Kilkerran Road
Campbeltown
Argyll, PA28 6JL
+44 (0) 1586 552133
info@ardshiel.co.uk
reservations@ardshiel.co.uk
www.ardshiel.co.uk

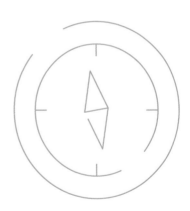

ST. COLUMBA

BRACE YOURSELF FOR A STUNNING COASTAL VIEW, FIERCE WIND, AND A HISTORIC CAVE.

▷ START AND END POINT	✕ DESTINATION
KEIL CAR PARK	**ST. COLUMBA'S FOOTPRINTS**

🏷 WHISKY	▦ DIFFICULTY
KILKERRAN FOR DISTILLERY VISITORS	**WALKING**

☆ HIGHLIGHTS	◷ DURATION OF THE HIKE
ST. COLUMBA'S CHAPEL, FOOT-PRINTS, HOLY WELL, VIEW OF NORTHERN IRELAND	**1.5 HOURS 3.4 MILES** (5.5KM)
	⋀ ELEVATION GAIN
	226 FEET (69M)

ALCOHOL **46 %** **CONTENT**

SINGLE MALT

KILKERRAN
GLENGYLE DISTILLERY
CAMPBELTOWN
Private Bottling
For
Distillery Visitors
2019
Single Malt Scotch Whisky
Distilled by Mitchells Glengyle Ltd.
Glengyle Distillery Campbeltown Scotland
PRODUCT OF SCOTLAND

LIGHT GOLD

FRUIT, MALT, GRASS

SPIC, PEAT, MALT

BOURBON CASK

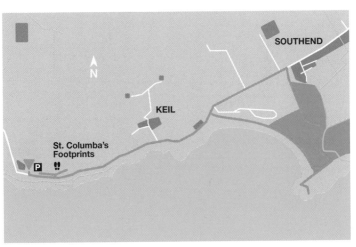

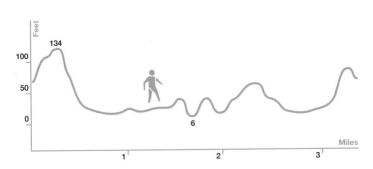

DESCRIPTION OF THE WALK

You will have to drive quite a bit to do this walk, but when you spot the otters you will know it was worth it.

Park at the Keil car park and walk to the cave and then up to the footprints of St. Columba. Continue along to St. Columba's well and then walk back to the road and head for the church ruins. Walk around and take in all the history and when you are ready head towards the beach. If you are lucky you can spot otters and even seals in the sea, frolicking around.

Walk towards the big rock and follow the turn-by-turn directions so you take the path the leads you to that road and back to the car park.

It is a good idea to bring lunch with you, especially if the weather is nice. That will give you some more time by the beach to watch the otters.

TURN BY TURN DIRECTIONS

Start from the Keil car park.

1. Walk left.
2. At 0.10 miles go left and immediately turn left again to get to the caves.
3. At 0.14 miles you arrive at the caves. Walk back along the same path.
4. At 0.19 miles continue forward and to St. Columba's footprints.
5. At 0.22 miles you will be at the footprints.
6. Walk further along the path to the holy well. Walk back to the road and go left.
7. At 0.44 miles you arrive at the church ruins.
8. At 1.03 miles turn right down the steps. Walk along the beach.
9. At 1.53 miles turn right towards Dunaverty rock.
10. At 1.68 miles you reach Dunaverty rock.
11. Go down again to the path and follow it, but at 1.83 miles walk straight ahead and follow the road back to the main road.
12. At 2.28 miles you reach the main road. Turn left.
13. Go back along the road towards the parking lot.
14. At 3.41 miles you arrive at the parking lot again.

KILKERRAN/GLENGYLE DISTILLERY

With this new distillery open, the town is well on its way back to its former glory. Campbeltown is still a long way from having the thirty-four distilleries it once had, but it is still a whisky town you should not miss out on.

This is the newest distillery in town and a sister distillery to Springbank distillery. Known as Kilkerran (but legally called Glengyle), this distillery is situated right next to Springbank Distillery.

Book tours online on the Springbank website. When you visit Kilkerran you can park at the Springbank parking area. If you have any questions regarding the booking, don't hesitate to give them a call; the staff are nice and helpful.

DRIVING DIRECTIONS

Kilkerran is at the same place as Cadenhead's and Springbank, in the middle of Campbeltown. You can find Keil carpark and St. Columba's footprints just off the B842.

PRACTICAL INFORMATION

DISTILLERY / WHISKY BAR
MITCHELL'S GLENGYLE LTD.
9 Bolgam Street
Campbeltown
Argyll, PA28 6HZ
+44 (0) 1586 552009
+44 (0) 1586 551710
info@springbank.scot
www.springbank.scot

RESTAURANT / CAFÉ
Bring a picnic.

MORE INFORMATION ABOUT THE AREA
www.explorecampbeltown.com

ACCOMMODATION OPTION
ARDSHIEL HOTEL
Kilkerran Road
Campbeltown
Argyll, PA28 6JL
+44 (0) 1586 552133
info@ardshiel.co.uk
reservations@ardshiel.co.uk
www.ardshiel.co.uk

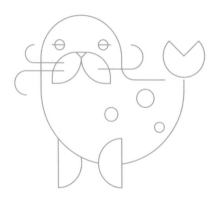

GLENRAMSKILL

A BEAUTIFUL WALK WITH A VIEW OF DAVAAR ISLAND

▷ START AND END POINT

ARDSHIEL HOTEL

✕ DESTINATION

GLENRAMSKILL

🏷 WHISKY

TAILS OF THE SEA
15 YO

🏛 DIFFICULTY

WALKING

☆ HIGHLIGHTS

VIEW OF DAVAAR ISLAND

🕐 DURATION OF THE HIKE

2.5 HOURS
6.2 MILES (10KM)

Λ ELEVATION GAIN

548 FEET
(167M)

ALCOHOL **56.6 %** CONTENT

SINGLE MALT

THE SCOTCH MALT WHISKY SOCIETY
ESTP THE VAULTS
LEITH, SCOTLAND

93.95   1 of 234

Tails of the sea

SINGLE MALT SCOTCH WHISKY • SINGLE CASK

15

56.6%VOL.70CL

- 👁 GOLD
- 👃 ANISEED, LAVENDER, SMOKE
- 👄 ORANGE, ANISEED, VANILLA
- 🛢 BOURBON BARREL

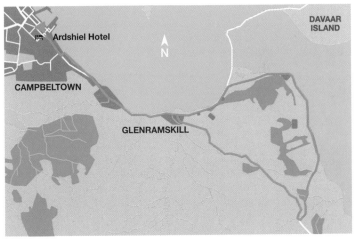

DAVAAR ISLAND

🏨 Ardshiel Hotel

N

CAMPBELTOWN

GLENRAMSKILL

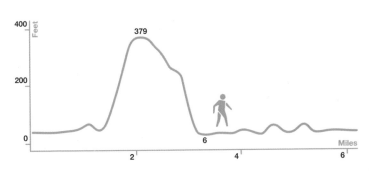

DESCRIPTION OF THE WALK

If you can tear yourself away from the hotel whisky bar (it's tough, I know), head out to the main road and follow the road on the right side. Go up a small road to the right after a couple of kilometres, walk through the gate, and follow the path. When you reach the electricity masts, turn right and walk on until you reach a gravel road that leads you to Le'arside Road. Go left here and as you follow the road towards town enjoy the spectacular view of Davaar Island. If you are doing this walk late in the evening, you might be able to spot some tourist stranded on the island, unable to return to the mainland until the water level retreats (I'm just kidding – but if you do the island walk at some point, make sure to keep a close eye on the water level so you don't get stranded).

The walk is about 10 km long and it is a nice one. It is lovely to be able to be so close to nature even when you are staying in a town.

The Scotch Malt Whisky Society is a society that originates in Scotland, but there are branches all over the world. Visit their website and find the one closest to you: *www.smws.com*. I tried one of their bottles, and their genius bottling of single-cask whiskies dazzled me. The goal of the SMWS is to go on a journey when you have a dram, to forget the concept of whisky brands, and to find new whiskies that you love. With funny names on the characteristically green bottles and an even funnier description of the whisky on their labels, they dare you to go out of your comfort zone and try something new.

TURN BY TURN DIRECTIONS

Start from the hotel.

1. Walk right down Kilkerran Road.
2. At 1.29 miles turn right and walk up the small road.
3. At 1.52 miles go through the gate.
4. When you reach the electricity masts, go right onto the path.
5. Follow the path with the fence on your left side.
6. At 2.03 miles you reach a larger gravel road. Turn right.
7. Follow the gravel road down to the main road Le'arside Road.
8. At 2.72 miles turn left.
9. Follow the road back to town.
10. At 6.23 miles you arrive at the hotel again.

ARDSHIEL HOTEL

I have met many whisky enthusiasts on my trip around Scotland. I myself have been called a whisky enthusiast, but the meaning of that word changed for me completely when I visited the Ardshiel Hotel. The owner clearly holds the title as the biggest enthusiast, and the hotel is a glorious sight to behold. Every wall is lined up with whisky bottles in the most fashionable way, and of course the whisky bar is also stocked to the brim.

When I started asking questions about the whisky, the owner was quickly fetched, and she kindly showed me around and told me everything about each bottle (every single one! I kid you not. It was amazing). She even challenged me and showed me a whisky bottle with no distillery name on it. It told a story about the fishing harbour, crabs, and smoked ducks. The distillery name is a secret that you must try and guess when tasting. Yes, I knew almost immediately. It was the taste and the style of one of my favourite distilleries, but she didn't know that.

For the whisky alone this is a place to visit, but the food is great as well, and they have lovely rooms.

DRIVING DIRECTIONS

You find Ardshiel Hotel on Kilkerran Road, just by the sea in Campbeltown.

PRACTICAL INFORMATION

DISTILLERY / WHISKY BAR
ARDSHIEL HOTEL
Kilkerran Road
Campbeltown
Argyll, PA28 6JL
+44 (0) 1586 552133
info@ardshiel.co.uk
https://ardshiel.co.uk

RESTAURANT / CAFÉ
ARDSHIEL HOTEL
(see information above)

MORE INFORMATION ABOUT THE AREA
www.explorecampbeltown.com

ACCOMMODATION OPTION
ARDSHIEL HOTEL
(see information above)

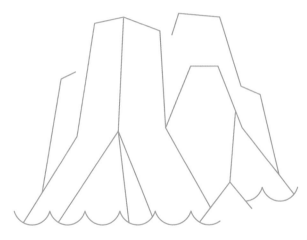

ARRAN

A COASTAL WALK WITH ICE CREAM ON THE WAY.

▷ START AND END POINT

ARRAN DISTILLERY

✕ DESTINATION

THE WHINS CRAFTS WORKSHOP

🏷 WHISKY

ARRAN
10 YO

🔠 DIFFICULTY

WALKING

☆ HIGHLIGHTS

COASTAL WALK, COASTAL VIEW, ICE CREAM

🕐 DURATION OF THE HIKE

2 HOURS
4.7 MILES (7.6KM)

∧ ELEVATION GAIN

492 FEET
(150M)

SINGLE MALT

ALCOHOL **46 %** CONTENT

👁	LIGHT GOLD
👃	FRUIT, HONEY, COCONUT
👅	MALT, FRUIT
🛢	BOURBON CASK SHERRY CASK

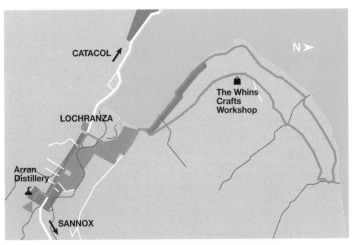

CATACOL

N ▶

The Whins Crafts Workshop

LOCHRANZA

Arran Distillery

SANNOX

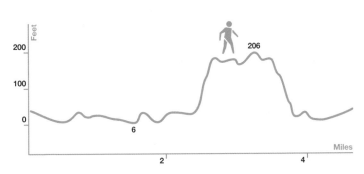

Feet

200

100

0

206

6

2

4

Miles

DESCRIPTION OF THE WALK

Arran is a gorgeous island with lots of walking trails. It is fun for the whole family. This walk has a special bonus: a craft workshop that sells ice cream, which really is a lifesaver on a hot day (oh yes, it can get hot in Scotland).

Park at the distillery. Let them know you are heading out and go on your way. Follow the main road and soon you will go right and walk towards the coast. Follow the turn-by-turn directions and head out on the path. It's a really nice and easy walk that the whole family can participate in.

On the top of a hill there is The Whins Crafts Workshop. Its opening times depend on the time of year. You can get lots of ice cream and beautiful objects here.

Continue and walk back to the main road and back to the distillery.

This walk can be done in all kinds of weather.

==== TIP ====

Arran is famous for its Isle of Arran ice cream, so what better time to try some than when visiting Arran?

TURN BY TURN DIRECTIONS

Start from the distillery.

1. Walk onto the main road. Turn left.
2. At 0.48 miles walk right and follow the road.
3. At 0.88 miles you reach the coast. Turn right.
4. At 1.45 miles the road turns into a path. Continue.
5. Follow the path along the coastline.
6. At 2.47 miles turn right and up the path.
7. At 2.89 miles the path becomes a gravel road. Continue.
8. At 3.38 miles you reach The Whins. Walk on.
9. At 3.88 miles go left. Walk along the road and follow it when it bends.
10. At 4.28 miles you reach the main road. Turn left and walk back to the distillery.
11. At 4.76 miles you have returned.

ARRAN DISTILLERY

Arran Distillery is a lovely distillery to visit. They have put a lot of effort into giving the visitors a great experience. And they do have a lot of visitors, so if you'd like to visit on a quiet day, give them a call and ask when the best time for a visit is. There are several different tours to choose from, all good and enlightening. If you want to book a tour, you can also book it on their website.

They have a great café where you can enjoy a bite before or after heading off on your walk or distillery tour.

DRIVING DIRECTIONS

To get to Arran you need to take a ferry.

PRACTICAL INFORMATION

DISTILLERY / WHISKY BAR
ISLE OF ARRAN DISTILLERS LTD
Lochranza
Isle of Arran, KA27 8HJ
+44 (0) 1770 830264
visitorcentre@arranwhisky.com
www.arranwhisky.com

Restaurant / Café
ISLE OF ARRAN DISTILLERS LTD
(see information above)

More information about the area
www.visitarran.com

Accommodation option
If you are not heading straight to the mainland
after visiting the distiller, have a look at this
website for tips on where to stay:
www.visitarran.com

Ferry
www.calmac.co.uk

BLADNOCH

TAKE A WALK ON THE WILD SIDE.

▷ START AND END POINT

BLADNOCH DISTILLERY

✕ DESTINATION

RIVER BLADNOCH

🏷 WHISKY

BLADNOCH ADELA
15 YO

🔡 DIFFICULTY

WALKING

☆ HIGHLIGHTS

RIVER WALK

🕑 DURATION OF THE HIKE

1.75 HOURS
4.2 MILES (6.7KM)

⌂ ELEVATION GAIN

138 FEET
(42M)

SINGLE MALT

ALCOHOL
46.7%
CONTENT

COPPER

CHERRY, RAISINS, CHOCOLATE

SHERRY, CHOCOLATE, COFFEE

OLOROSO SHERRY

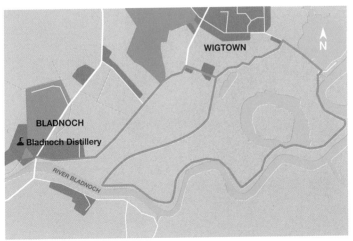

WIGTOWN

N

BLADNOCH

Bladnoch Distillery

RIVER BLADNOCH

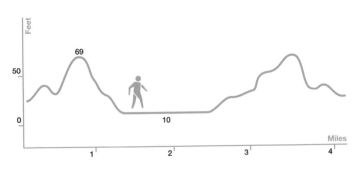

DESCRIPTION OF THE WALK

This is a brilliant walk where you meet a lot of cows and sheep along your way. They scare easily so it's best to let them be and admire them from afar.

Start at the distillery and walk up the road. Follow the turn-by-turn directions and soon you are walking on an embankment. The cows are also able to walk here but not as gracefully as you, so leave them be, as they might trip and fall when scared.

A little further, there is a picnic area where you can have lunch. There is a pub just across from the distillery, so if the weather is not friendly you can also eat there. Another option is the fancy new café in the distillery.

Follow the path along the River Bladnoch and soon you come to an old railway line; turn right here and follow the path. After that, just follow the turn-by-turn directions and soon you are back at the distillery hankering for a wee dram.

The distillery is close to Wigtown, which is an amazing little town full of bookshops, so if you have some spare time, you should pay it a visit.

TURN BY TURN DIRECTIONS

Start at the distillery.

1. Walk straight ahead up A714.
2. At 0.73 miles turn right.
3. At 0.85 miles go left on the path.
4. At 1.15 miles you reach a road. Turn right.
5. At 1.32 miles go right to a picnic area. Continue.
6. Follow the path alongside the River Bladnoch.
7. At 2.72 miles walk up to the old railway line and walk on its right along the path.
8. At 3.19 miles take the path to the left.
9. At 3.34 miles turn left.
10. At 3.46 miles you are back at the main road. Turn left.
11. At 4.20 miles you return to the distillery.

BLADNOCH DISTILLERY

This is an old distillery, but it was restored to its former glory not so long ago. When I visited, I could still smell the fresh coat of paint. They had just opened a few days earlier after being closed to the public due to renovation.

Bladnoch is unlike any other distillery I have visited. The decor in the visitor centre is very sleek and modern and the team of tour guides is very young but they know their whisky. The outer buildings look traditional but are renovated. The distillery has one tour of the distillery and it can be booked online on their website. You have to be above 14 years of age to go on the tour.

If you have questions or need help with the booking just give them a call, they are very nice and helpful.

DRIVING DIRECTIONS

You can find the distillery on the B7005 just south of Wigtown.

PRACTICAL INFORMATION

DISTILLERY / WHISKY BAR
BLADNOCH DISTILLERY
Bladnoch
Wigtownshire, DG8 9AB
+44 (0) 1988 402605
bookings@bladnoch.com
www.bladnoch.com

RESTAURANT / CAFÉ
CAFÉ MELBA AT BLADNOCH DISTILLERY
(see information above)

MORE INFORMATION ABOUT THE AREA
www.visitsouthwestscotland.com

ACCOMMODATION OPTION
SYKES COTTAGES LTD
Head office: One City Place
Chester
Cheshire, CH1 3BQ
+44 (0) 1244 356666
www.sykescottages.co.uk
info@sykescottages.co.uk

ANNAN

AN IDYLLIC RIVER WALK.

▷ **START AND END POINT**

DISTILLERY PARKING AREA

✕ **DESTINATION**

RIVERSIDE

🏳 **WHISKY**

MAN O'SWORD

▦ **DIFFICULTY**

WALKING

☆ **HIGHLIGHTS**

RIVER WALK

⊙ **DURATION OF THE HIKE**

2.5 HOURS
5.7 MILES (9.2KM)

△ **ELEVATION GAIN**

216 FEET
(66M)

ALCOHOL
61.6 %
CONTENT

SINGLE MALT

MAN O'
RDSWORDSW
ANNANDALE
SINGLE MALT SCOTCH WHISKY

👁	GOLDEN
👃	PEAT, FRUIT, APPLES, OAK
👄	SMOKE, CUSTARD, FRUIT
🛢	BUFFALO TRACE BARRELS

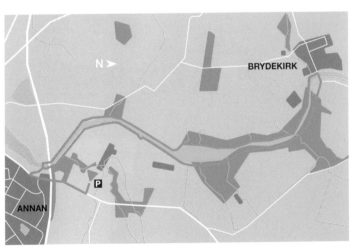

N ➤

BRYDEKIRK

P

ANNAN

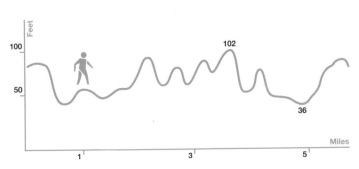

Feet

100

102

50

36

Miles

1   3   5

DESCRIPTION OF THE WALK

This was the last walk on our tour of Scotland and it wasn't easy. It is always difficult to plan these walks and whisky visits to make sure the weather is nice. When I did this walk, it was pouring down buckets of rain. We sought shelter at the Annandale Distillery, had a delicious lunch, and took an amazing distillery tour. Afterwards, the rain wasn't as bad and we finished the walk. You can do this walk in all kinds of weather, but we had to learn that sometimes it rains more than your waterproof gear can handle.

It is a gorgeous walk, the path along the river is crowded with trees which gives you a fairy-tale feeling.

Before you set out from the distillery, let them know that you are heading out and when you plan on returning. At the main road turn right, and when you reach the football club with the parking towards the river, head that way to the river and cross the metal bridge. Follow the river until you reach the stone bridge. Cross it and walk down the path to the right on the other side, and then head back towards the distillery.

The distillery has a brilliant café with lots of lunch choices.

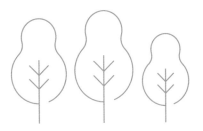

In Scotland there are invisible borders between five whisky regions. If one were to generalise (which one should not), each region has its own distinct whisky flavour. There is Lowlands (soft and smooth finish), Highlands (spicy, sweet, malty), Speyside (floral, sweet, and fruity finish), Islay (peaty, smoky, and malty), and Campbeltown (fruity and peaty). This might have been the predominant way back in the day, but things are changing, and more and more distilleries are breaking free from these old ways, invisible borders be damned.

TURN BY TURN DIRECTIONS

Start from the distillery parking.

1. Walk along the road and to the right.
2. At 0.45 miles turn right and you will come to a small parking lot. Walk down the path towards the water.
3. At 0.55 miles turn left and cross the bridge. Follow the path.
4. At 2.78 miles you reach a road. Go right.
5. At 2.91 miles cross the bridge and turn right down onto the path.
6. At 5.18 miles walk up towards the parking lot.
7. At 5.28 miles you arrive once again at the main road. Turn left.
8. At 5.73 miles you reach the distillery.

ANNANDALE DISTILLERY

Annandale Distillery is simply a joy to visit. The tours are funny and informative, and everyone is friendly and helpful. The team has a lot of plans in the works for making maps, for walks and hikes in the area so the visitors can combine whisky and walks. (It is no secret that I love that idea.) Because the site is old and difficult to access for disabled people, they are now working on a film screening option so that wheelchair users do not miss out on too much. Children can visit the distillery as well; there is no age limit. There are many different tour options, something for everybody. Give them a call and book the tour you would like to go on. And remember to tell them if you are using their parking space while walking; that way they know when to expect you back.

DRIVING DIRECTIONS

Annandale Distillery is just off the B722 north of Annan.

PRACTICAL INFORMATION

DISTILLERY / WHISKY BAR
ANNANDALE DISTILLERY
Northfield
Annan, DG12 5LL
+44 (0) 1461 207817
info@annandaledistillery.com
www.annandaledistillery.com

RESTAURANT / CAFÉ
THE MALTING COFFEE SHOP
AT THE ANNANDALE DISTILLERY
(see information above)

MORE INFORMATION ABOUT THE AREA
www.visitoruk.com/Annan

ACCOMMODATION OPTION
SYKES COTTAGES LTD
Head office: One City Place
Chester
Cheshire, CH1 3BQ
+44 (0) 1244 356666
info@sykescottages.co.uk
www.sykescottages.co.uk

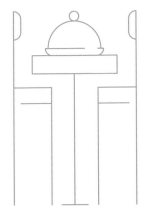

THANK YOU

I am not one for long thank-you speeches, in fact I am not one for speeches at all. But saying thanks is definitely due in this case so here goes:

Thank you to Hadi Barkat, CEO of Helvetiq, for giving this whisky-loving lass a chance to share the beauty of Scotland and the joy of whisky drinking with all the readers. Also, a big thank you to my very patient editor Satu Binggeli, you must be a saint to put up with me.

It goes without saying that I owe a big thank you to all the distilleries and whisky places that welcomed me and answered all my million questions; thank you so much.

A big thank you to my parents who helped with the kids while I was out in the wild getting lost and drinking whisky. Thanks to my kids for joining me on most of the trips to Scotland – they truly made it so much more fun. And finally, thank you to my husband for all his support and for being so easily lured into this Scotland adventure. I hope we have many more adventures to come.

4

INDEX

FIND A DISTILLERY

Whisky Walks Scotland
The Most Satisfying Way to Discover Scotland
By Maria Mazanti
ISBN 978-3-907293-66-9

Photos: Maria Mazanti & Asbjørn Sivertsen
Layout & illustrations: Daniel Malak, Elżbieta Kownacka, Anthony Pittet
Proofreading: Walter Smelt III, Karin Waldhauser
Printed in The Czech Republic

First edition 2022
Deposit copy in Switzerland: May 2022

helvetiq.com